Homeless to Homeowner Hero

The Inspiring True Story of a Real Estate Maverick

By

Kevin LaPlante

Homeless to Homeowner Hero by Kevin LaPlante
Copyright © 2024 - All Rights Reserved.

or indirect, that are incurred as a result of the use of the information contained within this document, including, but not limited to, errors, omissions, or inaccuracies.

No part of this publication may be reproduced or transmitted in any form or by any means, electronically or mechanically, except as permitted by law, without the copyright owner's written consent, except for brief segments quoted in a book review. The advice and strategies found within may not be suitable for some situations or is sold with the understanding that neither the authors nor the publishers are held responsible for the results curated from the advice in this book.

<u>About The Book</u>

"Homeless to Homeowner Hero" by Kevin LaPlante is an inspiring and transformative memoir that charts his extraordinary journey from living on the streets to becoming a successful homeowner and a professional realtor. This compelling narrative serves as both a personal triumph story and a practical guide for those aspiring to overcome adversity and achieve their dreams in the real estate world.

Kevin's story begins with his humble origins and the struggles that led to his homelessness. With candid honesty, he recounts the challenges he faced and the pivotal moments that ignited his determination to change his life. Readers will be captivated by Kevin's resilience as he navigates from a life without a permanent address to not only becoming a homeowner but also rising as a respected figure in the real estate industry.

The book is structured in two main sections. The first part tells the readers about the story of Kevin's personal life, tracing his path from homelessness to homeownership and beyond. It covers his early hardships, the risks he took, and the valuable lessons he learned as he entered the competitive real estate market. Kevin shares intimate details of his journey, from securing his first home to eventually scaling his business and establishing his own successful brokerage.

In the second section, Kevin distills the wisdom gained from his experiences into practical lessons for readers. He explores the power of mindset, the importance of personal branding, strategies for overcoming adversity, and essential tools for entrepreneurial success in real estate. Throughout, Kevin emphasizes that becoming a "homeowner hero" is not just about personal achievement, but also about using one's success to help others realize their dreams of homeownership.

"Homeless to Homeowner Hero" is not just any story. It's an inspirational tale of personal transformation; a testament to the power of perseverance and the American dream of homeownership. Kevin's journey proves that with the will to do something, the right mindset, work ethic, and guidance, anyone can overcome life's struggles and challenges, achieve their dream of becoming a homeowner, and even build a thriving career in real estate.

This book is an invaluable resource for aspiring homeowners, real estate professionals, entrepreneurs, and anyone seeking inspiration and encouragement to overcome life's challenges. Kevin's story serves as a beacon of hope and a practical guide for those looking to achieve homeownership and potentially build a career in real estate, regardless of their starting point. His personal and professional experiences will help the readers learn that true heroism lies in the courage to change one's life, the achievement of homeownership, and the dedication to helping others realize the same dream.

Contents

Kevin LaPlante

Section One

My Story

CHAPTER ONE

My Humble Beginnings in New Bedford, Massachusetts

I was born and raised in New Bedford, Massachusetts, a city known for its high crime rates and limited opportunities. My family of five—my parents, two older sisters, and myself—lived together in a cramped, three-bedroom apartment on the third floor of an old building. We never had the luxury of owning our own home or even dreaming of a better life. It was a constant struggle to make ends meet, with my dad being the sole breadwinner and working long hours at a tool factory.

Mom did her best to keep our family afloat, relying on Section 8 housing assistance and food stamps to ensure we had a roof over our heads and food on the table. Regardless of the challenges, we had what we needed, even if it meant living paycheck to paycheck. Looking back now, I realize the lessons of my childhood were truly invaluable - it taught me about perseverance through hard work, and the importance of cherishing family above all.

My relationship with my father was complicated. He was an alcoholic, which greatly affected our bond, however, I couldn't deny his work ethic and commitment. Day in and day out, he would wake up early and dedicate his 40 to 50 hours a week at the factory. Through witnessing his commitment, I gained an appreciation for perseverance through challenging times and the importance of dedication to one's work. His example instilled in me the value of perseverance and hard work, even when facing personal hurdles.

As I entered my teenage years, I felt an overwhelming urge to take some responsibility and contribute to my family's income to gain some financial independence. That's when my aunt stepped in and helped me land my first job at the age of 14. She called Rosie's, a local restaurant, every single day until they finally agreed to give me a chance as a dishwasher. I was thrilled to have the opportunity to earn my own money and prove myself in the workforce.

Starting my first job at such a young age was truly eye-opening. As a kid, I didn't take it very seriously at first. However, when I learned that the restaurant wasn't planning to keep me on after the summer, I stepped up my effort. I worked hard, learned quickly, and demonstrated my value to the team. By the end of the summer, not only did they decide to keep me, but I was also promoted to line cook - a major responsibility for someone of only fifteen years of age.

Working in the kitchen at Rosie's was a turning point in my life. I discovered my passion for cooking and thrived in a fast-paced environment. I loved creating delicious plates and basking in the energy of the restaurant industry. For three years, I honed my skills and absorbed knowledge from my older coworkers, gaining a glimpse into the real world beyond my peers.

Despite my success at work, I made a decision that would alter the course of my life. At 16, I dropped out of Greater New Bedford Regional Vocational High School. It was the time when I decided to dedicate more time to work to make more money, believing that it was the key to a successful future. In hindsight, I understand that this choice was shortsighted, but at the time, I was convinced that my street smarts and hustle would be enough to carry me through. Looking back, I realize that I had more gumption than brains. Still, all-in-all things eventually worked out well for me.

After leaving Rosie's at 17, I bounced around various restaurants and country clubs, seeking to expand my culinary expertise. By 18, I was a full-time cook, making a name for myself in the industry and refining my culinary skills. However, as I navigated the stressful and demanding world of the kitchen, I fell into a pattern of partying and reckless spending. Instead of saving the money I worked so hard to earn, I squandered it on nights out drinking and socializing.

It wasn't until a year or so later that I had a moment of clarity. I started to realize that if things didn't change, my life wasn't going to get better. I'd end up like so many others in my town, struggling to find good work and never having enough money. That's when I knew I had to try something new and leave New Bedford behind. It meant taking a chance on a future that was unsure. But staying the way things were wasn't a choice either. I needed to be brave and take that first step towards changing my story.

That's when I made the bold decision to move to New York City with my partner. With just $35 in my pocket and no concrete plan, I boarded a Greyhound bus to Times Square, ready to start a new chapter in my life. The first few months in the big city were a whirlwind of survival and hustle. I took on any job I could find, from cold-calling for the *New York Post* selling subscriptions to standing on street corners handing out flyers for promotions.

Living in The Big Apple on a shoestring budget taught me the importance of resourcefulness and resilience. I kept a meticulous record of every penny I borrowed, ensuring that I could pay back my debts and maintain my integrity. It was during this time that I began to develop a sense of responsibility and a hunger for something more.

A pivotal moment in my journey came when my partner landed a job with a real estate company called Foxtons. I watched with fascination as they provided a salary plus commission, something I had never encountered before. Intrigued by the potential of a career in real estate, I applied for a position at the company, eager to seize the opportunity.

Unfortunately, I was told that I was too young and lacked the necessary sales experience. They weren't interested in a 19-year-old with no experience. The rejection stung, but it also ignited a fire within me, leaving me with the thought that real estate was where I wanted to be, and I was determined to find a way to make it happen.

As I reflect on my humble beginnings in New Bedford and my early struggles in New York City, I realize that every challenge I faced served a purpose. Every problem and disappointment motivated me even more. They made me want to work hard and save so I could build a better life. The lessons from those years, like the value of hard work and taking chances, became the basics for everything good that happened later in real estate. I learned that if you push through hard times, they'll make you stronger and help you succeed in the future.

For those who find themselves in similar circumstances, feeling trapped by their environment or limited by their education, I want to offer a message of hope and encouragement. Your past does not define your future. You always have options and probably more options than you believe at the moment. Believe in yourself. With determination, resilience, and a willingness to take calculated risks, you can overcome even the most daunting obstacles and achieve your dreams.

As I started down my twisty road to real estate, I brought with me the lessons from my childhood and a big drive to do well. Don't forget - it's not where you began that matters, but where you decide to go. Be proud of humble starts, learn from your past, and use it to power you ahead. Challenges make us stronger if we push through and let them motivate us towards brighter days. With hard work, determination, and a willingness to seize opportunities, you too can transform your life and achieve the success you've always dreamed of.

CHAPTER TWO

My Winding Path to a Real Estate Career

It was the mid-2000s. I was in my mid-20s, returning to my home state after a transformative period of living and working in New York City. There was a time in my life when I dropped out of high school in ninth grade in pursuit of wealth and success. But now, having learned some hard and very valuable lessons. I was ready for a fresh start.

I found a little rental cottage in the town of Mattapoisett. It was a rural area, nestled in the middle of nowhere, but it felt like home. The cottage was just a small studio, part of someone's guesthouse, but it was mine for $850 a month. It was about a five-minute drive from my new job at a local diner called The Nest.

The Nest became my second home for the next three years. I started off as a cook, honing my skills in the fast-paced environment of the kitchen. I enjoyed the work, the camaraderie with my fellow cooks, and the satisfaction of serving up delicious meals to our customers. My hard work and dedication paid off when I was promoted to kitchen manager after just a year.

Unfortunately, The Nest eventually shut down so I was out of work again. But I didn't let that setback discourage me. As I wrote earlier, there are always options; you just have to go find them. I quickly found a position at Knucklehead's Bar & Grill, where I once again started as a cook before rising to the rank of kitchen manager. The job was good. I spent five years at Knucklehead's, and I can honestly say that the owners were some of the bests I've ever had in my life. They were very generous and genuinely cared about their employees. For example, if I was short $100 for my rent and explained my situation to them, they would give me an advance from my next paycheck to take care of my rent, so they really helped me out a lot. They almost treated every employee like family.

I was happy and satisfied with my job and my work place. However, despite the stability and support I found at Knucklehead's, I knew that I wanted more out of life and that at some time I'd have to move on. I had always dreamed of running my own business, and I realized that education was the key to making that dream a reality. So, while working full-time, I started taking classes to earn my high school equivalency diploma. It's important to understand that every challenge you face is balanced with the option of not accepting that challenge. Moving on and up or staying in place is a matter of choice. At such a crossroads, it's important to ask yourself which action (or non-action) will ultimately get you where you want to go in life. Which move is a step forward and which step holds you back? It's your call.

It wasn't easy for me to balance work and school, but my commitment and determination to succeed encouraged me to keep going. I enrolled in business classes at the local community college, soaking up knowledge about finance, management, and entrepreneurship. After years of hard work and dedication, I proudly earned my Bachelor's Degree in Business from Provident University. I can't explain the feeling of holding a degree in my hand. I really was proud of myself, not in an ego sense, but in the realization that I had set a tough goal under tough conditions and I had achieved it.

During this time, I also met the man who would later

become my life partner. It was 2013 and I was 26 years old. We connected online and quickly fell in love. He was young, only 19 or 20 at the time, and wasn't doing much with his life. He didn't even have a driver's license. I sat him down and had a serious talk with him, encouraging him to make something of himself. With my support, he ended up going to Job Corps and joining the army.

Little did I know that his decision would lead to a major upheaval in my own life. Just a few months after he completed basic training, I got a call from him saying, "You've got four days to move to Texas." He was being stationed in El Paso, and as his spouse, I needed to be there with him.

I packed up everything and drove 44 hours in four days from New Bedford to El Paso. It was a daunting journey, but I knew it was the start of a new adventure. When I arrived, I found myself selling flasks at the army base while I searched for more permanent employment. It was a humbling experience, but I was willing to do whatever it took to make ends meet. My aim was to demonstrate flexibility and determination during this transitional professional phase.

My big break came when I saw an ad for an assistant manager position at McDonald's. I applied, not expecting much, but to my surprise, they took a chance on me. The owner sat down with me for an interview and saw something in me that made him decide to give me the job.

Starting at the bottom as an assistant manager was fresh but a valuable experience. I learned so much about leadership, business, and managing people. I rose through the ranks, eventually becoming a general manager and running my own McDonald's store. At one point, I was responsible for managing up to 70 employees.

One of the highlights of my time at McDonald's was being sent to Hamburger University in Chicago. It was an honor to be chosen, as not many people get the opportunity. I spent a week there, learning about leadership and honing my skills. When I graduated, I received a diploma that read "Bachelor of Hamburgerology." It may sound silly, but it was a huge accomplishment for me.

My success at McDonald's caught the attention of a franchisee in Myrtle Beach, South Carolina. They recruited me to come to work for them, offering me a higher salary and the chance to take on a new challenge. I accepted the position and moved out there, but quickly realized that the demanding pace and high-stress environment weren't for me. Today, I enjoy the fast pace of real estate, but I find that the stress level is very low-key. When you really love your work, constant high levels of stress just don't exist.

After eight months, I called it quits and returned to my old McDonald's in Rhode Island. I had to take a step down to an assistant manager role, but I was grateful to have a job and the stability that came with it. That experience taught me the importance of knowing my limits and not being afraid to make a change when something isn't working. Knowing your limits doesn't mean you are constrained by those limits. You just have to be ready when you set out to expand them.

Throughout my journey, I learned that success doesn't come easy. You have to face challenges, setbacks, and other struggles every step of the way. But with hard work, determination, and a willingness to take risks, I was able to overcome every obstacle and build a life I could be proud of.

For those looking to follow in my footsteps and break into the real estate game, I have a few pieces of advice. First, *never stop learning*. Whether it's taking classes, attending workshops, or seeking out mentors, knowledge is power in this industry. Second, be willing to start at the bottom and work your way up. You won't always have a chance to get your desired role. So, don't be afraid to take on entry-level positions or grunt work, as those experiences will teach you valuable skills and help you build a strong foundation.

Finally, always remember that you will succeed if you're determined, no matter where you start. Take my story for an example; I dropped out of high school and spent years working in kitchens at different locations, but I never lost sight of my dreams. With hard work and perseverance, I was able to resume my education, earn my degree, build a successful career, and eventually break into the world of real estate.

As I look back on my winding path to a successful real estate career, I'm filled with a sense of pride and gratitude. Every step of the journey, from the late nights studying for exams to the long hours spent managing a team at McDonald's, played a role in shaping me into the person I am today. And now, as I embark on this new chapter as a real estate investor and entrepreneur, I'm excited to see where the road will take me next.

In the next chapter, we'll dive into the nitty-gritty of breaking into the real estate game. I'll share my experiences getting started in the industry, from obtaining my license to landing my first clients. Along the way, I'll offer practical advice and insider tips to help you navigate the world of real estate with confidence and success. So, let's turn the page and begin this exciting new journey together.

CHAPTER THREE

Breaking into the Real Estate Game

When my husband joined the army and got stationed at Fort Bliss in El Paso, Texas, we had to pack up everything and move there within just four days. With only $35 in my pocket when I first moved to New York years earlier, this cross-country move felt like "déjà vu all over again." But I knew how to adapt and make things work.

Soon after getting settled in El Paso, I joined an online group for Fort Bliss military spouses. Scrolling through posts one day, I spotted something that caught my eye. I saw that there were grants available for military spouses to cover the cost of real estate licensing classes. That was like a roadside sign reading "Successful Career Ahead." The opportunity jumped out at me. Real estate had always appealed to me ever since that real estate company in New York turned me down as a 19-year-old for being too green. But the timing hadn't been right before. Now I had years of experience as an entry-level employee, someone who had worked his way up to responsible positions and who had considerable experience in management. Best of all, living on base with housing covered and a bit of financial stability, I could actually pursue my dream.

Since everything seemed to be perfect, I applied right away for the $4,000 grant and was thrilled when I was approved. The funds opened the door for me to enroll in online classes through Champions School of Real Estate. Even better, their program was entirely virtual so I could complete it remotely. I hit the ground running, determined to finish as quickly as possible.

Buckling down, I managed to get through all six required real estate courses, totaling about 180 hours, in the span of just one month. It was a whirlwind, but I was eager and energized. Before I knew it, I was sitting for my national and state licensing exams. When I passed, it finally started to feel real—I was on my way to becoming a realtor.

Next came the challenge of choosing a brokerage to work under as I got my career off the ground. I interviewed at a few different places, knowing that finding the right fit would be key. Many of the brokerages operated on traditional commission splits between the agent and the company. But as a newbie, I was drawn to the 100% commission model at Realty One. Under their setup, agents simply paid a flat transaction fee to the brokerage for each deal rather than giving up a big cut of their commissions. I knew I'd need to hustle to drum up business, but I liked the idea of keeping more of the fruits of my labor.

Walking into the Realty One office on my first official day as a real estate agent, I was filled with a mix of nerves and excitement. The phone sat silently on my empty desk, not yet ringing with leads. It was up to me to make something happen. I poured myself a cup of coffee, took a deep breath, and got to work.

Before continuing with what I did, I want to share how I did what I did—a brief look at how to promote yourself and sell real estate based on the lessons, mistakes, and successes I've experienced throughout the years.

First, it's important to understand that as a real estate *professional*, you don't sell houses, buildings, or land. You sell what those properties provide for your clients and customers. A house isn't square footage in a good location with good schools;

it's a stable future in a great environment for raising a family. That building isn't a purchase; it's an announcement to the business world of your success in your area of expertise. It represents better service for your customers and a more comfortable and productive environment for your employees. That empty plot isn't just a piece of land; it's a future. It's whatever you can make of it. The adage about selling the sizzle and not the steak is directly applicable to real estate.

I know of a regional insurance firm, specializing in large food franchise accounts, that was looking to move from the firm's original office, a small, wooden structure in a rural setting. In the 80 or so years since the beginning of the firm, they had seriously outgrown that facility. Additionally, the old building was a poor representation of the firm's modern capabilities. One of the real estate agent's closing points in selling the new property dealt not with square footage, location, or utility rates, but with the enhanced image the new building would bring to the company.

Product knowledge is essential, and by selling that knowledge *through the eyes of the customer* you turn that knowledge into sales. "Mr. and Mrs. Smith, I know that a sound education is a primary concern. We all know that proper schooling is the road to success for our kids. I can assure you that our school system is among the finest in the state." (Follow up with statistics to back your statement.) That's the sizzle from that steak.

You want to build relationships with your customers. One, for possible repeat business. Two, for possible referrals to other customers. Three, for positive word of mouth in the community. Never underestimate the power of all three to enhance your career over the long term. The quality of the home, building, or property can't really speak for itself until it's been purchased and lived in or used. The relationship between you and the customer during the sale is in most ways the most important factor in concluding a sale.

"I'm new to real estate. Heck, man, I'm new to sales. How do I start?" you ask. First, give yourself a physical "once-over." Does the man or woman you see in the mirror look like someone you'd want to trust with your business? Is your dress appropriate to the business? Is your dress appropriate for the occasion? That, too, is a consideration. Conducting a sales tour of Johansen's Pig Farm in polished shoes and a three-piece wool suit during a summer heat wave might cast doubts about your common sense. Does that person in the mirror carry himself with confidence? Does he look comfortable in conversation and negotiation? If your answer is "yes," then you're ready to begin.

Attitude is key to success. Never underestimate the power of a warm smile, even in telephone conversations. Humans have an innate ability to sense a smile or a frown over long distances. Make sure your voice and tone carry your confidence and your friendly disposition. Doing your homework and really knowing your product enhances your confidence and your clients' trust in you, and it will show through in virtually everything you do and say. I've seen a lot of salespeople maintaining a "cool" attitude in a sales pitch. I think this is foolish. The prospect is excited about purchasing real estate. You should be equally excited about showing and eventually selling that real estate. Don't hold back. Show your excitement. It's catching.

I am guided by three fundamentals of sales: Attitude, enthusiasm, and goals; and selling strategies, which is a powerful combination, but long-term success requires the application of all three, and you need to master all three. Product knowledge is essential, but you'd be amazed at how many (unsuccessful) salespeople try to succeed without knowing even the basics of what they're selling. I've seen it happen. You have to know not only the property, but also the environment (business or family), where that environment is headed, and any other relevant factors to the sale. You can't sell it if you don't really know it, and I mean know it inside and out.

Core selling skills stem from one's interpersonal abilities. While extreme extroversion isn't essential for real estate success, confidence in your product knowledge and sincere focus on clients' needs can optimize outcomes. Goal-setting is imperative - without defining objectives, progress is unlikely. A constructive attitude combined with passion fuels planning. Consider your career aspirations, then map interim milestones to chart an actionable course toward your vision. With preparation and diligent effort, remaining ambitions become ever more tangible. Interacting compassionately while imparting expertise empowers clients. Translating ambitions into initiatives through incremental accomplishments cultivates career momentum. Maintain an adaptive, service-oriented approach on your professional journey.

I applied all that and more to my efforts in my environment. My market was clear—the massive military community at Fort Bliss. With over 40,000 soldiers stationed there and more rotating in all the time, there was a constant stream of folks in need of housing. That's practically an unending source of new prospects. Orders would come down, giving families just days or weeks to report to El Paso. Many were coming from overseas postings in places like Korea or Germany and had to secure a place to live sight unseen on tight timelines. I knew I could make their transitions easier and less stressful. That's a key attitude.

You're not so much selling property as you are making a challenging life experience more comfortable and even enjoyable.

I started by going all-in on social media, especially Facebook. With so many military spouses already connecting in groups there, it was the perfect place to get in front of potential clients. I kept in mind always that these individual people and families were traveling from different parts of the country and even entirely different countries to a new and probably challenging phase in their lives. My job as I saw it was to help make a major part of that move as easy as possible. I posted ads offering my services to help families relocating to Fort Bliss. My unique selling point? I'd go the extra mile by shooting video walkthroughs of rental houses and sale listings so those moving from afar could get a real feel for the property before committing. Virtual tours were a novelty at the time, and they're still an effective tool.

At first, business trickled in slowly but surely. I focused on rentals in those early days, which were faster transactions than sales. Working with a few initial clients allowed me to quickly rack up great reviews and testimonials, even though most hadn't met me in person. I made sure every review got posted prominently on my Facebook page. I'd ask happy clients to share feedback like "Kevin found me a great home!" or "I rented sight unseen from Kevin LaPlante and he made it so easy!" None of them needed to mention it was a rental deal. The aim was just to get my name out there and build credibility. Never underestimate the value of testimonials. Regardless of your confidence, your sales ability, and your efforts to build a relationship, the opinion of the outside objective observer is invaluable. The closing of the deal is an ideal time to ask for such a testimonial. Carry a voice recorder to make it easy for your customer. You can transcribe and edit later for use in your promotional materials.

Also, and this is key, closing is the best time to ask for referrals. "It has been a pleasure to serve you, Mr. and Mrs. Smith. Perhaps you know of someone in similar need." You'd be... you *will* be surprised at how effective this is.

As the positive word-of-mouth spread, my momentum picked up steam. More and more leads poured in from those Facebook groups. Military families started recommending me to each other, tagging me in posts whenever someone asked for realtor suggestions. I made sure to pounce on every opportunity. The common thread was that I understood their unique relocation challenges and had tailored my business to serve them. That's key. Again, you're not selling or renting a product; you are solving a serious problem.

I never stopped self-promoting. Every time I helped a new client find a home, I'd post about it online to keep attention on my growing track record and highlight my expanding success history. Closed another deal? Snap a photo with the happy buyers in front of their new place and post an announcement. Hit a sales milestone? Humblebrag about it and then go back to sharing more listings. I probably seemed like an eager beaver, but it worked. In my first six months as an agent, from June to December 2018, I made an impressive $145,000 within my first year in the real estate industry.

That success lit a fire under me to keep grinding.

The following year, I continued to focus on serving the military community at Fort Bliss. By consistently marketing my services on social media and delivering value to my clients, I was able to build a strong reputation as the go-to real estate agent for service members and their families. Word-of-mouth referrals played a significant role in the growth of my business, as satisfied clients recommended me to others in need of housing assistance.

All of this was made possible by recognizing an underserved community where my skills and hustle could add real value. Military life is full of uncertainties, but having a secure place to call home provides an anchor. It's about more than just four walls. By carving out that specialty for myself rather than trying to be a jack-of-all-trades generalist agent, I found my footing fast.

Now, I'm not special. I didn't finish high school. Heck, I didn't even make it through ninth grade. I grew up in a rough neighborhood and easily could've continued down a darker path. But I refused to let my lack of a high school diploma define me. Years later, I persevered and earned my GED, proving to myself that I had what it takes to succeed academically, even if it wasn't the traditional route. Ultimately, our destination matters more than steps along the way. Maintaining focus on long-term goals can empower transformation from humble beginnings through determination.

I got focused and bet on myself. Real estate gave me a way to channel my drive into helping people while writing my own paycheck. If I can do it, anyone can. It doesn't matter if you stumble in your early years or take an unconventional path. What matters is that you keep pushing forward, seizing every opportunity to better yourself and succeed, and create the life you want.

Maybe you find some similarities between my story and yours. Maybe you've felt counted out or behind the eight ball in life but still crave something more. Let my journey show you what's possible with the right mix of motivation, strategy, and old-fashioned work ethic. Understand too that this industry is demanding, requiring mental fortitude and resilience. There will be taxing days, problematic clients, and periods where revenue falls outside your control. Success stems from perseverance through obstacles as much as talent. Only by maintaining drive in the face of frustrations and disappointments can sustained career progress be made.

If you're not afraid of a little elbow grease and can keep the big picture in mind, a career as a realtor might be your ticket. Don't let a lack of formal education hold you back. The real learning happens out in the field. Find a customer base you're passionate about serving and get creative with your marketing. Build genuine relationships online and off.

Stay consistent even when it feels like you're not gaining ground. Generosity and grit will take you further than you ever imagined. Success doesn't happen overnight, but it does come to you when you refuse to give up. Three decades ago, I was a scrawny kid in El Paso just trying to figure out my next move. Today, I'm the broker-owner of 'Bliss Home Realty & Relocation Group' with more than 200 transactions under my belt. How does that sound?

The biggest piece of advice I can give is to take that first step before you feel totally ready. Nerves are normal. Mistakes are inevitable. But you'll never know what you're capable of unless you try. Real estate changed my life by giving me a career that pushes me to be better every day. If you're ready to take the leap, the next chapter will reveal how I went from solo agent to the head of my own firm. Keep reading to find out how to scale your business the right way.

CHAPTER FOUR

Scaling My Business and Branching Out

As my real estate career gained momentum, I found myself yearning for new challenges and opportunities to expand my horizons. With a consistent flow of clients and transactions coming in, I realized it was the perfect time to take my business to new heights. I had always been fascinated by the realm of commercial real estate and envisioned myself one day leading my own brokerage. However, before I could make that leap, I needed to broaden my knowledge and skill set.

In the early stages of my career, I had the opportunity to step into commercial real estate at my first company, but I didn't fully immerse myself in it. In retrospect, I regret not taking full advantage of the commercial side to gain more expertise. Nonetheless, commercial real estate remains an area of continued interest, which I aspire to develop a further understanding of in the years ahead.

I have always been an advocate for hands-on, real-world education over solely relying on "book learning." I vividly remember attending a university lecture and walking out midway through, realizing that I could gain more knowledge through practical experience rather than sitting in a lecture hall. This hands-on approach has been invaluable in my real estate journey, where each transaction presents unique challenges and valuable lessons.

First—a few general thoughts about the subject. Commercial real estate, especially small-business real estate, is the backbone of the US economy. Our ability for John Doe or

Mr. and Mrs. John Doe to start a business, purchase a piece of property for that business, or to expand that business, and thrive in that business is the envy of the world. And those of us in real estate are the people who are key to making all that happen. We're essential in creating the neighborhood grocery, automobile repair shop, local café, paperback bookstore, hardware store, dress shop, and... you name it and someone in real estate helped make it happen. Businesses need land and buildings. Customers need places to go to spend their money. Even online orders eventually lead to some physical location. That's where the real estate professionals enter the picture.

Commercial real estate and residential real estate may seem similar but operate very differently. For example, you won't find a tenant's bill of rights on the commercial end. Municipalities are more lenient generally towards the regulation of commercial properties. There are exceptions, of course, but as a rule, local governments realize the needs of a business tenant are significantly different from a family in need of a place to raise their kids. If you're in the market to become a landlord of commercial properties, you'll find that overall, you have considerably more flexibility in working with residential tenants. Overall, commercial real estate involves fewer regulations on things like rent rates and lease terms. This independence allows for customized arrangements fitting various business models. However, fewer tenant protections mean commercial landlords carry more responsibility too.

When purchasing commercial properties, you can expect to pay more cash up-front and to have more equity in the deal. Naturally, costs and rates vary from market to market and even from neighborhood to neighborhood, but as a general rule, commercial property payments run in the 25-30 percent area (as this is written). Overall, whichever area(s) you decide are best for you, it's a good idea to start small, gain experience, and develop a good reputation before jumping into major commercial ventures.

It bears repeating. As a real estate professional, you are in the business of solving problems for other people. The best way to help people is to help them make the right decisions. When someone is looking at a property, even a property they're sure they want, one that meets their needs, the sales professional will (surprisingly sometimes) find hesitation. It's natural, especially on big-ticket items such as commercial real estate. If you've really qualified your prospect and have shown the ideal property or properties, it's your obligation to help this potential buyer make the right decision. Remember, this person, this family, or this organization would not be investing so much time with you if they weren't serious about finding the right property.

That word "right" is key. I would never allow myself to sell the wrong property to a customer. One, basically, it's the wrong thing to do. Plus, word gets around. If you deal poorly or unethically with people, others will know. Bet on it. You'll lose business that never comes your way because of poor ethical standards. It's our duty as professionals to uphold the highest possible standards. This benefits not just the industry and the businesses, but also your individual reputations in the market. Doing excellent work builds trust with clients over time. It shows people they can rely on you to look out for their needs responsibly.

Deliver on your promises. I know an attorney who discovered a shocking fact when reading a survey about his industry. We all know about the reputation of lawyers, deserved or undeserved. "First, let's kill all the lawyers" is a famous literary phrase. What shocked the attorney was the fact that of all the problems and disappointments in dealing with that profession, their clients most resented the attorney or the firm for not responding to calls/text messages. I suspect many real estate clients share that feeling. What disappoints people most, it seems, is a basic lack of courtesy and respect. We're in this business for the long term, and that means building and maintaining longstanding relationships. Your client, customer, or prospect will never remember all the returned calls, but I assure you, they'll never forget the one you didn't. And that could be the call that may sink the deal. When you make a promise, even one as simple as making a phone call, *deliver.*

One of the most crucial steps I took in scaling my business was seeking guidance from a mentor. I have discovered that people are generally willing to lend a helping hand to others who are eager to learn and grow. You will find numerous real estate agents in your city or town successfully executing customer fix-and-flips. They will be more than happy to share their knowledge and guide you. I wish I hadn't let my pride hinder me from reaching out and asking for help whenever I needed it.

Pride can be a significant hindrance when it comes to personal and professional growth. There have been many instances where I had to set my ego aside and admit when I required guidance or assistance. However, every time I took that step, it yielded remarkable results. As I accumulated experience and established my business, I also recognized the significance of becoming a mentor myself. I wanted to offer the dedicated support and coaching that I wished I had received when I was just starting out in the industry.

In April 2022, I made a monumental decision and launched my own brokerage, Bliss Home Realty and Relocation Group.

It was an intimidating undertaking, but I felt confident in my abilities and readiness to take on this new challenge. I began with a single agent working alongside me, but within a matter of months, I expanded my team to seven talented people. In just eight months, I built a strong team of real estate professionals. We are planning to expand further this year. In the coming months, we will be relocating to a larger office space to accommodate the growth of the company.

Running my own brokerage has compelled me to cultivate a whole new set of skills, ranging from coaching and team building to emotional intelligence and people management. It has been a steep learning curve at times, but I am fully committed to providing the level of dedicated broker support that I didn't always receive when I was rising through the ranks in the industry.

I have always understood how challenging it can be when you first obtain your license and don't have a clear direction or someone to turn to for guidance. When you start with a company, they often try to assign you to a mentor, but this mentor usually has their own deals and responsibilities to handle, which can prevent them from training you effectively and providing the necessary support. It's possible that you will encounter one of those "this job'll kill ya, kid" types. You know the type; the bitter also-ran who blames his lack of success on anyone or anything other than himself. Don't listen to that garbage. You'll find successful, happy professionals all around you. Find them and hear what they have to say.

That's precisely why I make it a priority to personally mentor each of my new agents, offering one-on-one coaching and support to set them up for success. I am building a close-knit, family-oriented team where newly licensed agents can receive direct guidance from me. I provide hands-on broker support and don't pass them off to anyone else. I take it upon myself to train them and equip them with the tools they need to thrive.

Naturally, managing people comes with its own set of challenges. I have had to learn how to handle problematic employees and navigate difficult situations with tact and professionalism. The key is to sit down and have an open conversation with them. Perhaps they require additional training or coaching, or maybe it's something they inadvertently did that created the problem. I believe in giving people a chance and having a thoughtful discussion. It's also crucial to document everything, as there may come a time when parting ways becomes necessary. You may need that documented backup material to settle any dispute that comes up.

One of the most valuable lessons I have learned in scaling my business is the importance of identifying your niche and dominating it. When I first started out, I attempted to cater to everyone, but I quickly realized that this approach would lead to burnout and mediocrity. Instead, I chose to focus on becoming the go-to agent for military families relocating to the El Paso area.

I knew that working with military clients was my niche, and I excelled at it. To be honest, I consider myself somewhat of an introvert, so communicating with people over the phone wasn't my strong suit, especially in the beginning. However, working with military clients was advantageous because many of them were overseas, making the interaction more text-based. During downtime, I made sure to be consistent in my efforts to connect with them.

By concentrating on that specific market and delivering exceptional service to every client, I was able to cultivate a loyal client base and establish a strong reputation within the community. In March 2023, I was honored to be recognized as a top agent and featured in a national magazine. It was a proud moment and a testament to the dedication and hard work I had invested in my career.

As my business expanded, I also recognized the immense power of social media in building my brand and connecting with potential clients. I have established a substantial online presence, with more than 286,000 followers across various real estate groups and forums. There are times when, as a company owner and broker, I don't have all the answers. In those moments, I turn to these online communities to seek feedback and advice on how to approach certain situations.

Social media has also proven to be an invaluable tool for effectively marketing my listings and attracting new business. I make it a point to post consistently, diversifying my content with videos, flyers, and behind-the-scene glimpses into my work. I often advise other agents to consistently advertise their services, post videos showcasing homes, and create generic videos. The goal is to get people to know who you are and establish your presence in the market.

One of the most significant lessons I have learned throughout my real estate career is the importance of treating your agents well. I firmly believe that if you take care of your people, they will, in return, take care of your clients. That's why I offer generous splits and leads to my agents, even if it means occasionally taking a hit to my own bottom line. These little efforts of appreciation and support motivate them to go above and beyond for clients. Satisfied agents ensure satisfied clients through quality care. This reciprocal relationship has proven integral to our ongoing success in the market.

Currently, I invest approximately $3,500 per month in leads. My agents are thriving. Since many of them are fresh in the industry, this lead generation has been instrumental in helping them secure sales right from the start. However, I must admit that there are months when we do experience losses. But my agents work diligently and deserve the support, so I gladly provide it.

Throughout my journey, I have strived to remain humble and hungry, always eager to learn and improve. I recognize that success in this business is never guaranteed, and I must work tirelessly every day to earn the trust and respect of my clients.

One piece of advice I consistently share with new agents is to remain open to feedback and coaching, regardless of how much experience they gain. You can never be certain unless you have already collaborated with someone. Unfortunately, most of the time, joint ventures don't work out. It's a harsh reality, but it's the truth.

However, when you do find those rare gems—the mentors, partners, and team members who genuinely support you—cherish them and hold onto them tightly. Surround yourself with individuals who challenge you, uplift you, and believe in your vision.

As I reflect on my journey from a struggling kid in Massachusetts to a thriving real estate broker and business owner in Texas, I am filled with immense gratitude and pride. My story serves as a testament to the fact that with unwavering dedication, hard work, and a willingness to take risks, anyone can achieve their dreams in this industry.

To all the aspiring real estate agents and entrepreneurs out there, I want to emphasize this message: *Don't be afraid to dream big. Don't allow your past to dictate your future. And most importantly, never give up on yourself.*

If you want something badly enough, you will find a way to make it happen. I had a burning desire to be successful in life and I felt that getting out there, working hard, and earning money was more important than formal education. And when asked if I would advise young people today to follow the same path, my answer is a resounding yes. I know it may sound controversial, but later on, we can discuss how education, while valuable, is not the only path to success. You can go far with it, but it's not an absolute necessity.

With the right mindset, the right team, and the right strategies, you too can build a successful real estate business and create the life you've always dreamed of. It won't be a smooth ride, but I assure you, it will be worth every ounce of effort you put in.

Who knows? Perhaps one day, you'll be the one gracing the pages of a magazine, sharing your own success story and inspiring the next generation of real estate leaders.

As I contemplate my journey of scaling my business and venturing into new areas of real estate, I realize that this chapter of my life has been about so much more than simply generating income or closing deals. It has been a transformative experience of personal growth, leadership, and leaving a lasting impact on the real estate industry and the lives of those I work alongside.

Establishing my own brokerage and mentoring new agents has pushed me out of my comfort zone and challenged me in ways I never could have anticipated. It has compelled me to confront my own limitations and blind spots, constantly striving to better myself. But it has also shown me the incredible power of investing in people and helping others achieve their dreams.

I wholeheartedly believe that the key to long-term success in real estate (or any business) lies in building genuine relationships based on nothing but trust and providing value to others. Whether you're interacting with clients, agents, or industry partners, always aim to be someone who listens attentively, offers unwavering support, and goes the extra mile.

And remember, no matter how successful you become, stay grounded and never stop learning. The real estate industry is constantly evolving, and the moment you think you have all the answers is the moment you begin to fall behind.

So keep pushing yourself beyond your comfort zone. Keep seeking out new opportunities and challenges. And most importantly, keep giving back and uplifting those around you.

As I continue on my own professional journey, I am excited to delve even deeper into the world of real estate investing. In the next chapter, I will be sharing some of the hard-earned wisdom I have gained in navigating the intricacies of fix-and-flips, rentals, and beyond.

Whether you're just starting out or looking to strengthen your investing game and take it to new heights, I guarantee you'll find a wealth of actionable insights and strategies to help you achieve your goals. Ultimately, that's what this book is all about—empowering you to take control of your financial future and create the life you've always envisioned for yourself.

CHAPTER FIVE

A Few Words on Investing

In this chapter, I'll share the key lessons I've learned along the way, from choosing the right investment strategies to avoiding common pitfalls and identifying profitable niches. Whether just starting out or looking to advance, this information gives you what you need to achieve success in the rewarding field of real estate. Beginners gain useful tools, while more experienced investors find inspiration. Together these insights provide foundations and strategies applicable at any stage.

Many Options—don't try to do them all at once...

As a real estate investor, I've learned that there are numerous strategies to choose from when it comes to building wealth through property. From fix and flip to buy and hold, wholesaling to Airbnb rentals, the options can seem overwhelming at first. When I started my journey, I made the mistake of diving headfirst into a massive project—a 5,000-square-foot fix and flip on one acre of land. It was a daunting undertaking for a beginner, and I quickly realized that I had bitten off more than I could chew.

Looking back, I now understand the importance of starting with a smaller, more manageable project. For those just starting out, I recommend focusing on a three-bed, two-bath, 1,500-square-foot home. This size property allows you to gain valuable experience without getting in over your head. As you master the process and build confidence, you can gradually take on larger projects.

The key is to focus on one strategy at a time. Don't try to be a jack-of-all-trades; instead, become a master of one. Once you've honed your skills and achieved consistent success, you can consider diversifying your portfolio. And don't be afraid to seek guidance from experienced investors who have successfully implemented the strategy you're interested in. Their insights and advice can save you from costly mistakes and accelerate your learning curve.

One approach I recommend is partnering with a hard money lender. These lenders often have access to off-market properties that can be great deals for fix-and-flip projects. By building a strong relationship with a hard money lender, you can gain a competitive edge and secure profitable opportunities that may not be available to the general public.

Another crucial aspect of success in real estate investing is building a strong pipeline of leads. I recommend aiming for 50 to 100 prospects at any given time. This may seem daunting, but it can be achieved through consistent marketing efforts and networking. As you grow your pipeline, you'll have a steady stream of potential deals to evaluate and pursue.

Basics of Investing

To succeed as a real estate investor, it's essential to educate yourself on the fundamentals. This includes market analysis, property valuation, financing options, and legal considerations. Take the time to understand the different types of investments, such as residential, commercial, and land, and how they differ in terms of risk, return, and management requirements.

Develop a solid business plan that outlines your investment goals, target market, budget, and exit strategy. This will serve as your roadmap and help you stay focused and accountable. As part of your plan, build a strong network of professionals, including real estate agents, lenders, contractors, and attorneys. These relationships will be invaluable throughout the investment process, providing support, expertise, and resources.

One of the most important skills to master as an investor is analyzing deals and calculating key metrics. Learn how to determine cash flow, return on investment (ROI), and cap rate. These numbers will help you make informed decisions and identify the most promising opportunities. You can find numerous books, online resources, articles, lectures, and seminars on these and other key subjects, so, there's no need to get "into the weeds" here.

While my personal experience is primarily in residential real estate, I recognize the potential for higher returns and increased advertising opportunities in commercial investing. For example, you can put up large signs on high-traffic corner lots to promote your business and attract potential tenants or buyers. If you're interested in exploring commercial real estate, I recommend seeking out a mentor or joining a professional organization to gain insight and guidance.

Tips on Avoiding Red Flags

In the world of real estate investing, if a deal seems too good to be true, it probably is. Be cautious of opportunities that come with hidden risks or costs. Always thoroughly research the property, neighborhood, and local market conditions before making an investment. This includes inspecting the property in person and hiring a professional inspector to identify any potential issues or repairs that may impact your budget and timeline. Verify the seller's ownership and any outstanding liens or encumbrances on the property.

You don't want to find yourself in a situation where you're unable to close the deal or face unexpected legal challenges down the road. Be wary of high-pressure sales tactics or requests for upfront fees before closing the deal. Trust your instincts and don't be afraid to walk away from a deal that doesn't align with your investment goals or comfort level.

Another red flag to watch out for is joint ventures. While partnering with another investor can seem attractive, differing visions and styles can lead to conflicts and financial losses. I learned this lesson the hard way, losing quite a bit of money in a joint venture. What I discovered was that joint ventures rarely work out unless you have a proven track record of successful collaboration with your partner. If you do decide to pursue a joint venture, make sure to have clear agreements in place and a shared understanding of roles, responsibilities, and expectations.

Airbnb Investing

In recent years, short-term rental platforms like Airbnb have opened up new opportunities for real estate investors to generate passive income. If you're considering this strategy, look for properties located in popular tourist destinations or near major attractions. These areas tend to have higher occupancy rates and rental income potential.

However, before diving in, research local regulations and zoning laws related to short-term rentals. Some cities have restrictions or require special permits, so it's important to ensure compliance. Develop a detailed management plan that covers cleaning, maintenance, guest communication, and pricing strategy. This will help you ensure a positive guest experience and maximize your returns.

Airbnb offers valuable data and analytics tools that can help you optimize your listing, monitor performance, and make data-driven decisions. Utilize these resources to stay competitive and adapt to market trends. With the right property, location, and management approach, Airbnb investing can be a lucrative addition to your real estate portfolio.

Even Bad Markets Have Good Niches...

One of the most important lessons I've learned as a real estate investor is that even in challenging markets, there are always opportunities to find profitable niches. The key is to identify underserved segments and tailor your strategy accordingly.

In El Paso, Texas, there's a high demand for affordable housing near the military base. Many service members and their families are looking for convenient and budget-friendly options. By focusing on this specific niche and understanding the unique needs and preferences of military renters, I've been able to build a successful portfolio of rental properties.

Other niches to consider include student housing, senior living, or workforce housing. Stay attuned to local economic drivers, demographic trends, and development plans that may impact the demand and value of real estate in specific areas. By being strategic and adaptable, you can find opportunities to thrive in any market.

Another example of a profitable niche is land investing. A friend of mine bought two acres of land for $40,000 16 years ago. Today, without any improvements, that land is worth about $200,000. This demonstrates the potential for significant appreciation in land investments, particularly in areas where development is likely to occur.

When looking for land investment opportunities, I recommend focusing on areas where builders are currently developing. These areas are likely to continue expanding, and builders may be interested in purchasing land for future projects. By getting in early and holding onto the land, you can position yourself for substantial returns down the road.

Conclusion

Real estate investing has been a transformative journey for me. From humble beginnings, I've built a thriving career through hard work, determination, and continuous learning. The strategies and lessons I've shared in this chapter have been instrumental in my success, and I hope they provide valuable insights and inspiration for your own real estate investing endeavors.

Remember, success in real estate investing is not about having a formal education or a perfect background. It's about a willingness to learn, take calculated risks, and persist through challenges. By focusing on one strategy at a time, mastering the basics, avoiding red flags, exploring emerging opportunities like Airbnb, and identifying profitable niches, you can build a rewarding and impactful career in real estate.

As you embark on your own journey, don't be afraid to seek guidance from experienced investors, build strong relationships with professionals in the industry, and stay attuned to market trends and local opportunities. With dedication and a strategic approach, you can overcome obstacles and achieve your real estate investing goals.

In the next chapter "Lessons Learned," I'll share more of the meaningful insights gained through my career experience. You'll read personal stories and practical tips to help you handle the successes and challenges of real estate investing. We'll look at the mindset, habits, and strategies that can help propel your success in this enjoyable and rewarding field. My aim is to impart valuable perspectives to support your growth.

Section Two

Lessons Learnt from My Story

CHAPTER SIX

Lessons Learned

As I reflect on my incredible journey from a high school dropout to a successful real estate broker and business owner, I am overwhelmed with gratitude and awe. My path in this industry has been a rollercoaster filled with soaring highs and devastating lows. I have made my fair share of expensive mistakes but also achieved successes beyond my wildest dreams. The ups and downs, trials and tribulations have taught me so much about not just real estate, but also business, relationships, and life itself. My sincere hope is that by sharing the lessons I've learned, I can inspire and empower other ambitious people like me to boldly pursue their passions and dreams.

Perhaps the most impactful realization that I've had is that achieving big things in real estate does not require any fancy degree or formal education. Take my story as an example. I grew up in poverty in New Bedford, Massachusetts, and only made it through ninth grade before dropping out of high school at 16. My motivation was simple—I was eager to get out into the real world, work hard, and start making money to improve my circumstances. At the time, I believed that hustling and earning income was more valuable than completing my formal schooling. While I don't necessarily endorse that specific path, I do firmly believe that getting out there, gaining practical experience, and relentlessly applying yourself will beat an expensive degree any day.

My professional life began humbly in the restaurant

industry at just 14 years old. I started as a lowly dishwasher but quickly demonstrated my work ethic and value, ascending to line cook in short order. By the time I was 18, I was working full-time hours bouncing between various restaurants, soaking up all I could and sharpening my skills and instincts. Looking back, those early roles taught me so much about what it takes to make it in any field. Tireless hard work, being a team player, and an obsessive focus on pleasing customers—those are the fundamentals that I would carry with me into real estate and business down the line.

Another major lesson is the importance of taking bold, calculated risks. Nothing great is achieved by staying comfortable or playing small. For me, the greatest risk I ever took was moving to New York City at the age of 19 with a mere $35 in my pocket. As a small-town kid who had never stepped foot in a big city, it was positively terrifying. I had no safety net, no connections, and no idea how I would survive. But something in my gut told me that if I wanted to build an extraordinary life and career, The Big Apple was where I needed to be to make that happen.

I swallowed my fears, hopped on a Greyhound bus, and drove headfirst into the unknown. It was a daily struggle in those early days. I took any odd job I could find just to keep food on the table and a roof over my head. I pounded the pavement handing out flyers, did promotions for the *New York Post*, and scraped by on a tiny salary plus commission. It was far from glamorous, but that huge leap into uncertainty turned out to be the best decision I ever made.

Seeking out mentors and models of what's possible has also been instrumental to my growth. After learning about a real estate firm hiring agents with a base salary and commission, I eagerly interviewed with them. I had the enthusiasm and hustle, but I didn't have the sales experience they were looking for at that time. It was disappointing, but I didn't let that deter me. My partner ended up getting hired there, so I seized the opportunity to learn by osmosis, helping him out with researching properties and connecting with clients on the backend. I absolutely fell in love with the work and just knew deep down that real estate was my calling. That early exposure to working alongside an active agent gave me a priceless education I could never have gotten in a classroom.

One of the core philosophies that I drill into my team is this: 'People will do business with those they know, like, and trust. Real estate is first and foremost a relationships business. The agents who win aren't necessarily the slickest or most aggressive. They're the ones who focus on building genuine connections and proving their character, competence, and care to clients.'

Rather than just viewing leads as dollar signs, I teach my people to get face-to-face with prospects as quickly as possible and focus on being someone they would genuinely enjoy working with. When you prioritize being likable and trustworthy, the sales and referrals naturally flow from there.

With that said, there also comes a point in some deals when the most prudent thing you can do is walk away. I'm all for being relentless in the pursuit of making a deal work. But there are some clients and some terms that just aren't worth the headache and hassle. In any negotiation, you have to come up with a clear idea of what you're willing to accept and what crosses a line for you. I can't tell you how many times I've wasted time, energy, and heartache trying to appease completely unreasonable buyers and sellers. In some cases, you have two sides that are so entrenched in their demands and egos that the only sane solution is to cut bait. It stings in the short term, but your peace and freedom as a professional are worth more than any single stubborn deal.

Another hard-won insight that I've learned is about knowing when to stop selling. I've seen green agents who finally get a client to the finish line, but then proceed to keep talking and pushing well past the point of commitment. The result is they end up accidentally talking the buyer out of a decision they were already sold on! Real art is guiding a prospect to a choice in such a natural way that saying "yes" feels like the only logical conclusion. It's about easing into an agreement, not bludgeoning them over the head with persistence. If you find yourself struggling to close smoothly, I highly recommend practicing active listening and mirroring back what matters most to the client. When they feel truly heard and understood, getting to "yes" is almost effortless.

Possibly my greatest differentiator in this business has been my willingness to leave money on the table. I know that sounds counterintuitive in a commission-driven industry. But some of the wisest advice I ever got was *"don't be greedy."* In my experience, giving up a slice of your commission for the sake of the client and deal ends up coming back to you many times over.

In my early days, I easily sacrificed $20,000 in commissions by shaving down my side to help military families get into homes. It was a financial hit at the time. It was also the honorable thing to do. And it ended up creating an army of raving fans who sent me so much repeat and referral business over the years that it more than made up for it. My philosophy is if you spend your days helping others achieve what they want, you'll wake up one day realizing you have everything you want, too.

Now, in case you think my journey has been nothing but a smooth ride, let me assure you I have failed spectacularly and often. Anyone who tells you that you can succeed big without facing big setbacks is selling you a fantasy. Some of my most ambitious ventures have gone down in flames, leaving me reeling and wondering how I would recover. House flipping has been especially humbling. On my first attempt, I got in way over my head and overspent on a massive fixer-upper that bled me dry. It was an exhausting two-year ordeal that I narrowly crawled away from by selling at a huge loss. To say it was an expensive education in biting off more than I could chew would be a massive understatement.

But I didn't let that experience destroy my dreams. I objectively analyzed my mistakes—taking on too big a project, not having a clear budget—and applied those hard-won lessons to my next deals. The two flips after that were home runs because I downsized my scope and got religious about sticking to a budget. I share this not to brag but to illuminate an all-important truth: Failure is unavoidable and inevitable if you're in the arena reaching for big things. What separates those who go the distance from those who give up is how you respond to failure. You can't let it infect your mind and confidence. All you can do is dispassionately dissect what went wrong, integrate the lessons, and then keep marching forward with even more clarity and resolve.

Mindset is the linchpin that holds it all together. I truly believe that 90% of success is just maintaining a relentlessly positive, proactive, and persistent outlook. People are always commenting that I have a permanent smile on my face. It's not that I don't have challenges and frustrations like everyone else. I've just conditioned myself to always look for the solution, silver lining, and path forward rather than dwelling on problems. Staying upbeat and optimistic is what allows me to show up and go to work day in and day out even when external circumstances look bleak. I treat my mindset and mood like the most important business assets I have because in many ways they are.

So much of high achievement comes down to visualization and walking in faith before you have any concrete evidence to justify it. I call it accomplishing your goals in your mind first. You have to be able to feel the emotions of your victory before you can create it in reality. Every great feat begins as a vivid image and inspiration in the mind. You can't stop there. You have to match that inner certainty with nonstop action and effort. I can't count how many 16-hour days I've put in, following up with every lead and preparing for a breakthrough moment that I had no guarantee would arrive. But because I held fast to that mental picture of my best life, it pulled me forward until one day I woke up and realized I was here.

A dangerous trap I see far too many agents and entrepreneurs fall into is becoming complacent and stagnant. In the beginning, they're ravenous to learn and grow. But once they achieve a certain level of success, it's tempting to put things on cruise control and get a little too comfortable. I have to remind myself and my team that this impulse spells death for a real estate business. Markets can turn on a dime and customer needs are always evolving. I've had to pivot and adapt so many times over my career to stay ahead of shifting conditions. What was working brilliantly six months ago can become completely obsolete without warning today. Adopting a beginner's mindset and committing to being a lifelong learner is how you insulate yourself from irrelevance and thrive in any market.

On the topic of continuing to grow, I also can't overstate the importance of staying humble and hungry no matter how far you rise. From the outside looking in, some might assume I'm content to rest on my laurels. After all, I'm a high school dropout who cracked the code and built a seven-figure empire doing millions in transactions a year all while growing my own firm. I've graced the covers of industry magazines and been honored with just about every award there is. By conventional standards, I have *"made it."* But something in me will never be satisfied with coasting or settling. I'm on fire to keep stretching myself, expanding what I'm capable of, and seeing how many people I can help. The day I'm not excited to jump out of bed and get after it is the day I know something is very wrong.

Through it all, the one factor that I keep coming back to is the power of relentless persistence. I firmly believe that a huge percentage of success is just refusing to quit on yourself or your vision. If I had thrown in the towel after that first soul-crushing flip, I wouldn't be where I am today. Looking back, I'm so grateful for all the struggles, mistakes, and dark nights because they made me who I am. The greatest triumphs are always preceded by the greatest tests. And the sweeter the dream, the more obstacles there will be on the path. But if you commit in your heart to just keep putting one foot in front of the other no matter what, you will stun yourself with how far you can go. I'm a walking, talking, deal-closing case study for this.

So perhaps the ultimate lesson is this: Your beginnings do not determine your endings. I came from poverty and dysfunction, bounced around low-paying jobs, and didn't even finish 9th grade. By every predictive factor, I should have remained stuck and small, like so many around me did. But I decided to bet on myself and pursue my highest vision, even when it made no logical sense. I stumbled constantly, made a million mistakes, and wanted to give up more times than I'd like to admit. But my "why" and the person I knew I could become were always bigger than my challenges and fears. Slowly but surely, I turned my life into a masterpiece far grander than my limited origins could have predicted.

You can think of building your real estate career like crafting the most delectable gourmet meal. It starts with getting clear on your desired outcome and assembling the very best ingredients and tools you can access. But that's just the beginning. The real magic happens in the messy, imperfect process of combining those components through trial and error. Even the greatest chefs scorch a few dishes and need to modify their recipes as they go. The key is learning from those misfires and continually course-correcting rather than calling it quits. Because with enough patience and practice, you develop an instinct for how flavors blend together to create something transcendent. And it's in the repetition of showing up meal after meal, service after service, that you discover your own special sauce that has people lining up for a taste.

What I most want to imprint on you is that the story of your past and circumstances does not have to be the story of your future. I am living, breathing, commission-cashing, customer-satisfying proof that a person can completely reinvent themselves and rise above any odds or adversity. But make no mistake, it takes a deep belief in yourself, voracious learning from mentors, taking bold leaps before you're ready, and being willing to fail your way forward. Making a fortune in real estate has given me freedoms and options I still can't fully comprehend. But more than that, it's given me the platform to elevate others and demonstrate what becomes possible when you align your mindset and actions around a purpose bigger than yourself. If a poor kid from New Bedford can take these principles and completely transform his trajectory, I know beyond a shadow of a doubt that you're capable of the same.

So, it's time to get into the kitchen of your calling and start experimenting, tasting, and trusting the process of your own success recipe. Will you make a mess and have some batches that fall flat at first? Almost certainly. But if you learn to treat those as valuable lessons rather than stop signs, you'll refine your offering into something irresistible and inimitable. Stepping up to the banquet of your dreams isn't for the faint of heart—it's for those who are willing to bet on themselves and keep going no matter what life serves up. And if you're still reading this, I suspect that's exactly who you are. As you take these ideas and run with them, always know that I'm rooting for you and standing as evidence for how sweet the victory can be. Cheers to you, my friend, and go cook up a life and business beyond your wildest imagination!

CHAPTER SEVEN

Building Your Personal Brand

Defining Your Unique Value Proposition

In today's competitive world, building a personal brand is essential for standing out and achieving success. Whether you are an entrepreneur, a professional, or a freelancer, your personal brand is a reflection of who you are, what you stand for, and the value you bring to others. At the core of a strong personal brand is a unique value proposition (UVP) – a clear statement that defines what makes you different and why people should choose you over others. Defining your UVP is the foundation of building a compelling personal brand that resonates with your audience and sets you apart from the competition.

A unique value proposition is a succinct statement that highlights your strengths, skills, and the benefits you offer. It communicates your unique qualities and the specific value you bring to your target audience. Crafting a UVP involves self-reflection, understanding your audience, and articulating your distinct attributes in a way that is clear, compelling, and memorable.

The first step in defining your UVP is *self-reflection*. Understanding your strengths, passions, and values is crucial. Take the time to assess your skills, experiences, and accomplishments. What are you good at? What do you enjoy doing? What are the core values that guide your actions and decisions? By answering these questions, you can identify the unique qualities that set you apart.

When I began my career in real estate, I faced a lot of competition. To define my UVP, I reflected on my journey and identified the skills and experiences that made me unique. I realized that my perseverance, adaptability, and ability to connect with clients on a personal level were my strongest assets. My background of overcoming adversity and my commitment to providing exceptional service became the foundation of my UVP.

Once you have a clear understanding of your strengths and values, the next step is to *understand your target audience.* Knowing who you want to reach and what they need is essential for crafting a UVP that resonates with them. Consider the characteristics, preferences, and pain points of your target audience. What challenges do they face? What are their goals and aspirations? By understanding your audience, you can tailor your UVP to address their specific needs and demonstrate how you can provide value.

In my real estate business, I focused on military families relocating to new areas. I knew that their primary concerns were finding affordable housing quickly and minimizing the stress of moving. By understanding their needs, I was able to craft a UVP that highlighted my expertise in helping military families find homes efficiently and with minimal hassle. This focus on a specific audience allowed me to differentiate myself from other realtors and build a strong personal brand.

Articulating your UVP requires clarity and conciseness. Your UVP should be a brief, compelling statement that communicates your unique qualities and the benefits you offer. It should be easy to understand and memorable. Avoid jargon and complex language; instead, use simple and direct language that resonates with your audience.

When crafting your UVP, consider the following structure:

1. Identify your target audience: *Who are you serving?*

2. Highlight your unique qualities: *What makes you different?*

3. Communicate the benefits: *What value do you provide?*

For example, my UVP in real estate could be articulated as: *"I help military families find affordable housing quickly and with minimal stress, leveraging my personal experience and deep understanding of their unique needs."*

Your UVP should be authentic and reflect your true self. It's tempting to exaggerate or embellish your qualities to stand out, but authenticity is key to building trust and credibility. Be honest about your strengths and experiences, and let your genuine personality shine through. People are drawn to authenticity, and a UVP that accurately represents who you are will resonate more deeply with your audience.

Storytelling is a powerful tool in defining and communicating your UVP. Sharing your personal story can illustrate your unique qualities and create an emotional connection with your audience. Stories are memorable and can make your UVP more relatable and impactful.

In my journey, I often share my story of moving to New York City with just $35 in my pocket and building a successful real estate career through perseverance and hard work (I have shared this story over and over again, I'm sure you have also read this story and you'll still get to read again as you move on in this book... haha). This story not only highlights my resilience and determination but also connects with clients who may be facing their own challenges. By weaving your story into your UVP, you can create a narrative that showcases your strengths and makes your brand more compelling.

Consistency is another critical element in building your personal brand and reinforcing your UVP. Your UVP should be consistently reflected in all your communications and interactions, from your website and social media profiles to your business cards and elevator pitch. Consistency builds recognition and trust, making it easier for people to remember you and understand the value you offer.

For instance, if my UVP emphasizes helping military families find homes, all my marketing materials, social media posts, and client interactions should reflect this focus. Consistently delivering on my UVP reinforces my brand and strengthens my reputation in this niche.

Feedback is invaluable in refining your UVP. Seek feedback from colleagues, mentors, and clients to ensure that your UVP accurately represents your strengths and resonates with your audience. Be open to constructive criticism and be willing to make adjustments as needed. Feedback can provide valuable insights and help you fine-tune your UVP to make it even more compelling.

Building a personal brand is an ongoing process that evolves over time. As you gain more experience and your career progresses, your UVP may need to be updated to reflect new skills, achievements, and market trends. Regularly revisiting and refining your UVP ensures that it remains relevant and continues to resonate with your audience.

Defining your unique value proposition is a crucial step in building a strong personal brand. It involves self-reflection, understanding your target audience, and clearly articulating your unique qualities and the value you provide. By crafting a compelling UVP, you can differentiate yourself from the competition, connect with your audience, and build a personal brand that stands out. Remember to be authentic, use storytelling to illustrate your strengths, maintain consistency in your communications, and seek feedback to refine your UVP. With a well-defined UVP, you can confidently navigate the competitive landscape and achieve your personal and professional goals.

Leveraging Social Media and Digital Marketing

Now, I want you to pay utmost attention to this section. A lot of people only use WhatsApp, Facebook, Instagram, LinkedIn, and other social media platforms for fun and messages but these platforms are the gold mine they have refused to see. I'm gonna be showing you how you can use these social media platforms to your advantage to create wealth for yourself.

In today's digital age, social media and digital marketing have become indispensable tools for building and promoting your personal brand. Leveraging these platforms effectively can amplify your reach, engage your audience, and establish your presence in your industry. Understanding how to use social media and digital marketing to your advantage is crucial for anyone looking to stand out and achieve success. Here's how you can harness the power of these tools to build and enhance your personal brand.

Understanding Your Audience

The first step in leveraging social media and digital marketing is to understand your audience. Knowing who you are trying to reach will help you tailor your content and strategy to meet their needs and preferences. Consider the demographics, interests, and behaviors of your target audience. What platforms do they use? What type of content do they engage with? Understanding your audience will allow you to create more relevant and compelling content that resonates with them.

When I started building my personal brand as a real estate agent, I knew my primary audience consisted of military families relocating to new areas. I researched their online behavior and discovered that many of them used Facebook and Instagram to stay connected with family and friends and find local services. This insight helped me focus my efforts on these platforms and create content that addressed their specific needs and concerns.

Choosing the Right Platforms

Not all social media platforms are created equal. Each platform has its unique strengths and audience. Choosing the right platforms for your personal brand is essential for maximizing your reach and engagement. Here's a brief overview of some popular platforms:

Facebook: Ideal for building a community and engaging with a diverse audience through posts, videos, and groups.

Instagram: Great for visual storytelling, showcasing your personality, and connecting with a younger demographic.

LinkedIn: Best for professional networking, sharing industry insights, and establishing thought leadership.

Twitter: Useful for sharing real-time updates, engaging in conversations, and connecting with influencers.

YouTube: Perfect for creating and sharing video content, tutorials, and vlogs to engage a wide audience.

By focusing on the platforms where your audience is most active, you can create a more effective and targeted social media strategy.

Creating Compelling Content

Content is the heart of social media and digital marketing. To build a strong personal brand, you need to create compelling content that provides value to your audience. This content should be informative, engaging, and aligned with your unique value proposition. Here are some tips for creating effective content:

Be Authentic: Share your personal experiences, insights, and stories. Authenticity builds trust and makes your content more relatable.

Provide Value: Offer useful information, tips, and advice that address your audience's pain points and interests.

Use Visuals: High-quality images, videos, and graphics can significantly enhance the appeal of your content and increase engagement.

Be Consistent: Regularly posting content helps maintain your audience's interest and keeps you top of mind.

Engage with Your Audience: Respond to comments, messages, and feedback. Engaging with your audience fosters a sense of community and loyalty.

When I first started using social media to promote my real estate services, I focused on creating content that addressed common challenges faced by military families during relocation. I shared tips on finding affordable housing, managing the stress of moving, and navigating new communities. This content not only provided value but also positioned me as an expert in my niche.

Utilizing Digital Marketing Strategies

Digital marketing encompasses a range of strategies beyond social media that can help you reach a broader audience and achieve your branding goals. Here are some key digital marketing strategies to consider:

Search Engine Optimization (SEO): Optimize your website and content for search engines to increase visibility and attract organic traffic. Use relevant keywords, create high-quality content, and ensure your site is user-friendly.

Email Marketing: Build an email list and send regular newsletters to keep your audience informed and engaged. Personalized emails can build stronger relationships with your audience.

Content Marketing: Create and distribute valuable content across various channels to attract and retain a clearly defined audience. This can include blog posts, articles, videos, and infographics.

Paid Advertising: Invest in targeted ads on platforms like Google, Facebook, and Instagram to reach a wider audience and drive traffic to your website or social media profiles. This is really important because you have to spend money to make more money. You mustn't be reluctant to spend your money to drive more people towards to see what you are doing and spend their money on it when they see how it benefits them.

Analytics: Use analytics tools to track your performance, understand your audience's behavior, and refine your strategies based on data-driven insights.

One of the most effective digital marketing strategies I used was email marketing. By building an email list of potential clients and sending regular newsletters with valuable content and updates, I was able to maintain engagement and keep my audience informed about my services. You must have also experienced how several businesses keep sending you mails and the likes, it is a way of sensitizing your mind, and then converting you into their priceless customer in the long run. Additionally, using SEO techniques helped improve my website's ranking on search engines, driving more organic traffic and leads.

Building a Community

Social media is not just about broadcasting your message; it's about building a community. Engaging with your audience, participating in conversations, and fostering a sense of connection can create a loyal and supportive community around your personal brand. Here are some ways to build and nurture your community:

Start Conversations: Ask questions, create polls, and encourage discussions to engage your audience.

Join Groups and Forums: Participate in relevant groups and forums where your target audience is active. Share your expertise and build relationships.

Host Live Sessions: Use live video sessions to interact with your audience in real time, answer questions, and provide valuable insights.

Collaborate with Influencers: Partner with influencers and other professionals in your industry to expand your reach and credibility.

In my real estate business, I joined several online groups and forums where military families sought advice and support. By actively participating in these communities and offering helpful advice, I was able to build strong relationships and establish myself as a trusted resource.

<u>Consistency and Patience</u>

Building a personal brand through social media and digital marketing takes time and consistent effort. It's important to be patient and persistent. Results may not be immediate, but with consistent effort and a clear strategy, you will see growth over time. Stay committed to providing value, engaging with your audience, and refining your approach based on feedback and analytics.

Leveraging social media and digital marketing is essential for building and promoting your personal brand. By understanding your audience, choosing the right platforms, creating compelling content, utilizing digital marketing strategies, and building a community, you can amplify your reach and establish a strong presence in your industry. Remember to stay authentic, provide value, and be patient in your efforts. With dedication and strategic use of these tools, you can achieve your personal and professional branding goals and stand out in today's competitive landscape.

CHAPTER EIGHT

Marketing and Sales

In the world of real estate, both marketing and sales are the lifeblood that keeps our dreams alive and our businesses thriving. As I sit here, highlighting my journey from a high school dropout to a successful real estate broker, I can't help but feel a surge of emotion. The path I've traveled has been paved with countless challenges, moments of self-doubt, and exhilarating triumphs. But through it all, one thing has remained constant: the power of effective marketing and sales strategies to transform lives and build empires.

Let me take you back to where it all began. Picture a young, scrappy kid from New Bedford, Massachusetts, with nothing but a burning desire to make something of himself. I didn't have a fancy education or a network of connections to fall back on. What I did have was an unwavering belief that I could create my own destiny. Little did I know that this belief would become the foundation of my approach to marketing and sales in the real estate industry.

When I first stepped into the world of real estate, I was a fish out of water. I watched as seasoned agents effortlessly closed deals and built impressive client lists. For a moment, I felt overwhelmed and out of my depth. But then I remembered the lessons I'd learned in those early days of hustling in New York City. Success wasn't about having the most polished resume or the fanciest degree. It was about connecting with people on a human level and showing them that you genuinely cared about their needs.

This realization was the spark that ignited my passion for marketing and sales in real estate. I understood that at its core, our business isn't about properties or transactions – it's about people and their dreams. Every home we sell, and every investment we facilitate, is a stepping stone towards someone's vision for a better life. And it became my mission to not just sell houses but to sell hope, security, and the promise of a brighter future.

With this mindset, I dove headfirst into developing my marketing and sales strategies. I knew I couldn't compete with the big players in terms of advertising budgets or established reputations. But what I could offer was authenticity, dedication, and a willingness to go above and beyond for my clients. I decided to make these qualities the cornerstone of my personal brand.

One of the first lessons I learned was the importance of storytelling in marketing. People don't just buy properties; they buy into stories. They want to envision themselves living in that cozy suburban home, raising a family, and creating memories. Or they dream of owning that sleek downtown condo, symbolizing their success and cosmopolitan lifestyle. I realized that my job wasn't just to list features and square footage, but to paint vivid pictures of the lives my clients could lead in these spaces.

I began crafting compelling narratives for each property I listed. Instead of dry, factual descriptions, I wove tales of sun-drenched mornings in the breakfast nook, of cozy evenings by the fireplace, of backyard barbecues with friends and family. I wanted potential buyers to feel an emotional connection to the property before they even stepped through the door. And you know what? It worked. Properties that had been sitting on the market for months suddenly started attracting interested buyers.

But storytelling wasn't just about the properties – it was also about me. I knew that in a sea of real estate agents, I needed to stand out. So I started sharing my own story – the story of a kid from a tough background who refused to let his circumstances define him. I opened up about my struggles, my failures, and my eventual successes. I wanted my clients to see me not just as an agent, but as a real person who understood the value of hard work and perseverance.

This vulnerability in my marketing approach was terrifying at first. I worried that people might judge me for my lack of formal education or my humble beginnings. But to my surprise, it had the opposite effect. People were drawn to my authenticity. They saw in me someone who could relate to their own struggles and aspirations. Suddenly, I wasn't just another agent trying to make a sale – I was a partner in their journey towards achieving their dreams.

As my business grew, I discovered the power of niche marketing. In El Paso, I noticed a significant population of military families who were often overlooked by other real estate professionals. Many of these families faced unique challenges – frequent relocations, tight timelines, and the need for a stable home environment amidst the uncertainties of military life. I saw an opportunity to not just serve this community, but to become their go-to expert in real estate matters.

I immersed myself in learning about the specific needs of military families. I studied military relocation processes, familiarized myself with VA loans, and even learned the lingo used in military circles. Then, I tailored my marketing efforts specifically to this niche. I created informational videos addressing the common concerns of military homebuyers. I wrote blog posts offering tips on how to make a house feel like home even during short-term assignments. I even started a Facebook group where military families could connect and share advice about living in El Paso.

The response was overwhelming. Word spread quickly through the military community about an agent who truly understood their unique situation. I started receiving calls and messages from service members stationed all over the world, seeking guidance on buying or selling homes in El Paso. It wasn't just about closing deals anymore – I had become a trusted advisor, a friend, and sometimes even a confidant to these families during one of the most stressful periods of their lives.

This experience taught me a valuable lesson about the power of specialization in marketing. By focusing on a specific niche and truly becoming an expert in serving their needs, I was able to build a loyal client base that not only brought me repeat business but also became my most enthusiastic advocates.

But marketing isn't just about attracting clients – it's also about nurturing relationships and providing value long after the sale is complete. I made it a point to stay in touch with my clients, checking in on them regularly, sending thoughtful gifts on special occasions, and providing useful information about home maintenance, local events, and market trends. This approach not only led to repeat business but also generated a steady stream of referrals.

I remember one particular client, a young couple buying their first home. They were nervous, overwhelmed by the process, and unsure if they were making the right decision. I took the time to walk them through every step, explaining things in simple terms and always being available to answer their questions. Even after the sale was complete, I continued to check in on them, offering advice on home improvements and connecting them with reliable contractors.

A year later, I received a call from the husband. His voice was filled with emotion as he told me that they were expecting their first child. He wanted my help in finding a larger home for their growing family. But more than that, he wanted to thank me for being there for them during a pivotal moment in their lives. He said that my support had given them the confidence to take that first step towards homeownership, which had set them on a path to building the life they had always dreamed of.

Moments like these remind me why I got into this business in the first place. It's not about the commissions or the accolades – it's about the lives we touch and the dreams we help realize. And that's what effective marketing and sales in real estate should be all about – connecting with people on a deep, emotional level and becoming a trusted partner in their journey.

As my business grew, I realized the importance of leveraging technology in my marketing efforts. Social media, in particular, became a powerful tool in my arsenal. I saw it not just as a platform for promoting listings, but as a way to build a community and showcase my personality and values.

I started creating content that went beyond just real estate. I shared personal stories, offered glimpses into my daily life, and even showed my vulnerabilities and challenges. I wanted my followers to see the real me – not some polished, perfect version of a real estate agent, but a genuine person who was passionate about helping others achieve their goals.

This approach resonated with people. My social media

following grew, and I started receiving messages from people who felt like they knew me, even though we had never met in person. They appreciated my honesty and felt a connection to my story. When it came time for them to buy or sell a home, I was the first person they thought of.

But social media was just the beginning. I embraced video marketing, creating virtual tours of properties that allowed potential buyers to explore homes from the comfort of their own living rooms. This became especially valuable during the COVID-19 pandemic when in-person viewings were limited. I even started a YouTube channel where I shared tips on home buying, selling, and real estate investing. These videos not only showcased my expertise but also helped me reach a wider audience beyond my local market.

Technology also allowed me to streamline my sales process. I invested in customer relationship management (CRM) software that helped me keep track of leads, follow up with clients, and provide personalized service at scale. This meant that even as my business grew, I could maintain the same level of attentiveness and care that had been the hallmark of my service from day one.

But with all this technology at our fingertips, I never lost sight of the human element in sales. I believed – and still believe – that nothing can replace the power of a face-to-face conversation, a firm handshake, or a genuine smile. So while I embraced digital tools, I always made sure to balance them with personal interactions.

I made it a point to meet with clients in person whenever possible. I would invite them for coffee, not to hard-sell them, but to genuinely get to know them and understand their needs.

These conversations often went beyond real estate – we'd talk about their families, their dreams, their fears. And in these moments, I wasn't just a real estate agent – I was a confidant, a friend, someone they could trust with one of the biggest decisions of their lives. This approach to sales – blending high-tech tools with high-touch personal service – became my signature. It allowed me to scale my business without losing the personal connection that had been the foundation of my success.

As my reputation grew, I faced a new challenge – managing a team of agents and instilling in them the same passion for marketing and sales that had driven my success. I knew that simply teaching them techniques and strategies wouldn't be enough. I needed to inspire them, to help them find their own authentic voice in this competitive industry.

So I started mentoring sessions where I shared not just my successes, but also my failures and the lessons I learned from them. I encouraged my team to embrace their unique stories and experiences, to find their own niches, and to approach sales not as a transaction, but as a way to make a positive impact on people's lives.

I remember one agent on my team, Sarah, who was struggling to find her footing in the industry. She was shy and uncomfortable with the idea of 'selling' herself. During one of our mentoring sessions, I asked her to tell me about why she got into real estate. Her eyes lit up as she talked about her passion for historic homes and her dream of helping preserve the architectural heritage of our city.

That's when I saw the spark – the same spark that had ignited my own passion for this business years ago. I worked with Sarah to develop a marketing strategy that showcased her expertise in historic properties. We created a blog where she could share the stories behind some of the city's most iconic homes. We organized walking tours of historic neighborhoods, with Sarah as the guide.

Slowly but surely, Sarah found her confidence. She wasn't just selling houses anymore – she was sharing her passion and knowledge with others. And people responded. She became known as the go-to agent for historic properties in our area. Watching her transformation reminded me of the transformative power of authentic marketing and purpose-driven sales.

As I look back on my journey in real estate marketing and sales, I'm filled with a sense of gratitude and awe. I think about that scared kid from New Bedford who didn't even finish high school, and I marvel at how far I've come. But more than that, I'm amazed by the lives I've been able to touch along the way.

I think about the first-time homebuyers I've guided through the process, watching their eyes light up as they receive the keys to their very own home. I think about the families I've helped relocate, easing their transition to a new city and a new chapter in their lives. I think about the investors I've advised, helping them build wealth and secure their financial futures.

Each of these experiences has reinforced my belief in the power of marketing and sales done right. It's not about slick tactics or pushy techniques. It's about building relationships, adding value, and genuinely caring about the outcomes for your clients.

As I write this, I'm reminded of a quote by the great Maya Angelou: *"People will forget what you said, people will forget what you did, but people will never forget how you made them feel.*" This, I believe, is the essence of effective marketing and sales in real estate – and in life.

To those of you reading this who are just starting out in your real estate journey, or perhaps considering a career in this field, I want you to know that you have the power to make a real difference in people's lives. Your marketing efforts can be more than just advertisements – they can be beacons of hope for people searching for their dream homes. Your sales skills can be more than just closing techniques – they can be the bridge that helps people cross from aspiration to achievement.

Don't be afraid to bring your whole self to this business. Share your story, your passion, your why. Be authentic in your marketing, and be genuine in your sales approach. Remember that behind every transaction is a person with hopes, dreams, and fears. Your job is not just to sell properties, but to guide people towards a better future.

And when you face setbacks – because you will – remember my story. Remember that success in this industry isn't about where you came from or what degrees you hold. It's about your willingness to learn, adapt, persevere, and most importantly, care deeply about the people you serve.

As I conclude this chapter, I want to leave you with a challenge. Tomorrow, when you sit down to craft your next marketing message or prepare for your next sales call, pause for a moment. Think about the lives you have the potential to impact. Think about the dreams you have the power to help realize. Let that be your driving force.

Because at the end of the day, that's what truly matters in this business. It's not about the number of listings you have or the size of your commission checks. It's about the families you've helped find their perfect homes, the investors you've guided towards financial freedom, and the communities you've helped build and strengthen.

That's the true measure of success in real estate marketing and sales. And it's a success that's available to each and every one of you, regardless of your background or circumstances. So go out there, tell your story, share your passion, and make a difference. The world is waiting for what you have to offer.

CHAPTER NINE

Time Management and Productivity Tips

The most valuable asset in the world is not land or houses or this or that. The most valuable asset you can have in your possession is time. Reflecting on my journey from a high school dropout to a successful real estate broker and entrepreneur, I can't help but feel a swell of emotion. The path I've walked has been anything but straight, filled with twists, turns, and more than a few stumbling blocks. But through it all, one thing has remained constant: the relentless ticking of the clock. Time, that most precious and irretrievable of resources, has been both my greatest ally and my most formidable adversary.

I remember those early days in New Bedford, Massachusetts, when every minute felt like an eternity. Growing up in poverty, surrounded by limited opportunities, I yearned for a way to fast-forward through the hardships and into a brighter future. Little did I know then that the key to unlocking that future lay not in wishing time away, but in learning to harness its power.

When I dropped out of high school at 16, driven by an insatiable hunger to make money and change my circumstances, I thought I was taking a shortcut. In reality, I was embarking on a journey that would teach me the true value of time. Those long hours in restaurant kitchens, scrubbing dishes and flipping burgers, were my first real lessons in time management. Every second counted, every moment was an opportunity to prove my worth and climb the ladder.

As I stand here now, successful beyond my wildest dreams, I

can't help but feel a deep sense of gratitude for those early struggles. They forged in me a respect for time that has been the cornerstone of my success. And it's this hard-won wisdom that I want to share with you now, dear reader. Because no matter where you are on your journey, whether you're just starting out or well on your way, mastering the art of time management and productivity can be the difference between merely dreaming and actually achieving.

Let me paint you a picture of a typical day in my life now. The alarm blares at 5 AM, and I'm up before the first rays of sunlight peek through my window. There's a moment, brief but potent, where the old me wants to hit snooze and roll over. But that moment passes quickly, replaced by a surge of excitement for the day ahead. Because I know that these early morning hours are golden, a gift that I give myself each day.

As I lace up my running shoes and head out the door for my morning jog, I can feel the world around me slowly coming to life. The streets are quiet, the air crisp and full of possibility. This is my time to think, to plan, to set my intentions for the day ahead. With each footfall, I'm not just exercising my body, but sharpening my mind, preparing it for the challenges and opportunities that await.

Back home, showered and energized, I sit down to my most important task of the day: my morning routine. This isn't just about checking emails or scrolling through social media. No, this is a sacred time, dedicated to personal growth and self-reflection. I write in my gratitude journal, listing three things I'm thankful for. I meditate for 10 minutes, clearing my mind and centering myself. And I review my goals, both short-term and long-term, recommitting myself to the path I've chosen.

It's amazing how this simple routine, taking no more than 30 minutes, sets the tone for my entire day. By the time I walk into my office at 8 AM, I feel like I've already accomplished so much. And in a way, I have. I've won the first and most important battle of the day – the battle against procrastination and self-doubt.

Now, I know what you might be thinking. "That's all well and good for you, Kevin. But I'm not a morning person. I can barely drag myself out of bed, let alone go for a run and meditate!" And to that, I say: I wasn't always a morning person either. This routine, like all good habits, was built over time, with patience and persistence. The key is to start small. Maybe for you, it's setting your alarm 15 minutes earlier. Maybe it's just taking five minutes to write down what you're grateful for before you start your day. The specifics don't matter as much as the commitment to investing in yourself and your time.

As the day unfolds, I move through my tasks with a sense of purpose and focus that I could only have dreamed of in my younger years. I use a system I call "time blocking" to structure my day. Each hour is dedicated to a specific task or category of tasks. From 9 to 11, I might be making calls to potential clients. From 11 to 1, I'm in meetings with my team. The afternoon might be split between property viewings and administrative work.

This system isn't about rigidity – it's about creating a framework that allows for both productivity and flexibility. Because let's face it, in the real estate world (and in life), unexpected things happen. A client might call with an urgent request. A deal might fall through at the last minute. By having a clear structure to my day, I can more easily adapt to these curveballs without letting them derail my entire schedule.

One of the most powerful productivity tools I've discovered is the power of saying "no." In the early days of my career, I said yes to everything. Every client, every meeting, every opportunity. I thought that's what it took to be successful. But all I was doing was spreading myself too thin, diluting my effectiveness, and burning myself out.

Learning to say no was hard. It went against every instinct I had, every lesson I'd learned about hustling and grinding. But it was also liberating. By saying no to the things that weren't aligned with my goals or values, I was able to say a bigger, more emphatic yes to the things that truly mattered.

I remember the first big opportunity I turned down. It was a lucrative deal, one that would have padded my bank account nicely. But it also would have required me to compromise on my ethics, to cut corners in a way that didn't sit right with me. As I sat across from the client, my heart racing, I heard myself say, "I'm sorry, but I don't think this is the right fit for me."

The silence that followed felt like it lasted an eternity. But at that moment, I felt a shift inside me. I realized that by valuing my time and my principles, I was valuing myself. And that, more than any deal or dollar amount, was priceless.

Now, don't get me wrong. Saying no doesn't mean being closed off to opportunities. It means being discerning, being intentional about how you spend your time and energy. It means understanding that every yes comes with an implicit no to something else.

This brings me to another crucial aspect of time management and productivity: the importance of prioritization. In my office, I have a large whiteboard where I write down my top three priorities for the week. Not ten, not five, but three. These are the big rocks, the things that if accomplished, will move the needle in my business and my life.

Everything else – the emails, the minor tasks, the busy work – those are the pebbles. They'll find their way into the gaps, but they don't drive my day. By keeping my focus on these top priorities, I ensure that I'm always moving forward, always making progress on the things that truly matter.

I learned this lesson the hard way. There was a period in my career when I was busier than ever, working longer hours than I had since my restaurant days. But despite all this activity, I felt like I was standing still. I was confusing motion with progress and busyness with productivity.

It took a moment of brutal honesty with myself to realize what was happening. I was allowing myself to get caught up in the small stuff, the urgent but not important tasks that ate up my time and energy. I was reacting to every ping of my phone, and every new email in my inbox, instead of proactively shaping my day.

The change didn't happen overnight. It took conscious effort and constant reminders to stay focused on what really mattered. But the results were transformative. Not only was I accomplishing more, but I felt a sense of control and purpose that had been missing before.

One tool that's been invaluable in this journey is the art of delegation. As someone who came from nothing, who had to fight and claw for every opportunity, letting go of control wasn't easy. I had this deeply ingrained belief that if I wanted something done right, I had to do it myself.

But as my business grew, I realized that this mindset was

holding me back. There simply weren't enough hours in the day for me to do everything. More importantly, by trying to do everything, I was robbing myself of the time and energy to focus on the things that only I could do – the high-level strategy, the relationship building, the vision casting.

Learning to delegate was a process of trust – trust in my team, trust in the systems we'd put in place, and ultimately, trust in myself as a leader. It meant investing time upfront to train and empower my staff, to create clear processes and expectations. But the payoff has been enormous. Not only has it allowed me to reclaim my time, but it's also given my team opportunities to grow and develop their own skills.

I remember the first big project I fully delegated to one of my team members. As I watched her take ownership, bringing her own ideas and perspective to the table, I felt a mix of pride and amazement. Here was someone taking what I had built and making it better, expanding what was possible in ways I hadn't even imagined.

That's the beauty of effective time management and productivity. It's not just about getting more done in less time. It's about creating space for growth, for innovation, for the kind of big-picture thinking that can take you and your business to the next level.

Of course, no discussion of productivity would be complete without talking about the role of technology. We live in an age of unprecedented connectivity and access to information. Used wisely, technology can be an incredible amplifier of our productivity. But used carelessly, it can become a black hole, sucking away our time and attention.

I've experimented with countless apps and tools over the

years, always on the lookout for that perfect system that would solve all my time management woes. But what I've discovered is that the tool itself is less important than how you use it. The most sophisticated project management software in the world won't help if you don't have the discipline to stick to your priorities.

That said, there are a few tech tools that have become indispensable in my daily routine. *My calendar app* is my external brain, keeping track of appointments and deadlines. A simple note-taking app on my phone captures ideas and insights throughout the day, ensuring that no flash of inspiration is lost. And a task management app helps me keep track of my to-do list, allowing me to prioritize and reprioritize as needed.

But perhaps the most important tech tool in my arsenal is the 'Do Not Disturb' function on my phone. In a world of constant notifications and alerts, carving out periods of uninterrupted focus is crucial. When I'm working on a high-priority task, my phone goes into Do Not Disturb mode. Those emails and messages will still be there when I'm done, but for that block of time, I'm able to give my full attention to the task at hand.

As I've grown older and (hopefully) wiser, I've come to appreciate the importance of balance in productivity. There was a time when I equated productivity with constant motion, with filling every moment with activity. But true productivity, I've learned, requires periods of rest and reflection.

That's why I make sure to schedule regular breaks throughout my day. A 10-minute walk around the block to clear my head. A quick meditation session between meetings to recenter myself. These aren't indulgences or wastes of time –

they're investments in my mental clarity and overall effectiveness.

I also make it a point to disconnect completely at regular intervals. Once a quarter, I take a full week off – no email, no phone calls, no work of any kind. It's not always easy. The first couple of days, I often feel antsy, my mind racing with all the things I "should" be doing. But by the end of the week, I return to work refreshed, brimming with new ideas and perspectives.

This practice of stepping back has taught me a valuable lesson: sometimes, the most productive thing you can do is nothing at all. By giving your mind space to wander, to make connections, and to see the bigger picture, you open yourself up to insights and breakthroughs that might never come in the midst of constant activity.

As I wrap up this reflection on time management and productivity, I'm struck by how far I've come from that scrappy kid in New Bedford who thought success was about working harder, faster, and longer than everyone else. Don't get me wrong – hard work is still a crucial ingredient in the recipe for success. But it's not about grinding yourself into the ground. It's about working smarter, about leveraging your time and energy in ways that align with your goals and values.

I think about the young people I mentor now, many of whom remind me of my younger self. They're hungry, they're driven, they're ready to take on the world. And while I admire their enthusiasm, I also try to impart the lessons I've learned about the true nature of productivity.

I tell them that time management isn't about squeezing more tasks into each day. It's about making space for what truly matters. It's about being intentional with your time, treating each moment as the precious, non-renewable resource that it is.

I encourage them to reflect on their definition of success. Is it just about making money? Or is it about creating a life of meaning, of impact, of fulfillment? Because true productivity, I believe, is about aligning your daily actions with your deepest values and aspirations.

To those of you reading this, wherever you are on your journey, I want you to know that mastering your time is within your reach. It doesn't require special talents or superhuman discipline. It simply requires a commitment to valuing yourself and your time, and to making conscious choices about how you spend your days.

Start small. Choose one area of your life where you feel time slipping away from you. Maybe it's those aimless hours scrolling through social media. Maybe it's saying yes to commitments that don't truly serve you. Whatever it is, make a commitment to change it, not overnight, but gradually, consistently.

Remember, every master was once a beginner. Every productive person you admire once struggled with procrastination and was overwhelmed. The difference is that they decided to take control of their time, rather than letting time control them.

As you embark on this journey of mastering your time and productivity, be patient with yourself. There will be setbacks. There will be days when you fall back into old patterns. But don't let those moments discourage you. Instead, view them as opportunities to learn, to refine your approach, and to recommit to your goals.

And above all, never forget why you're doing this. Time

management isn't about becoming a productivity robot, ticking off tasks with ruthless efficiency. It's about creating a life that reflects your values, that allows you to pursue your passions, and that gives you the freedom to make a difference in the world.

For me, mastering my time has allowed me to build a successful business, yes. But more importantly, it's allowed me to be present for my family, to give back to my community, and to continually grow and evolve as a person. It's allowed me to write this book, to share my story, and hopefully inspire others to reach for their dreams.

As I look back on my journey, from those long nights in restaurant kitchens to the cover of industry magazines, I'm filled with a profound sense of gratitude. Gratitude for the lessons I've learned, for the opportunities I've been given, and for the time I've been blessed with.

And so, I leave you with this final thought: Your time is your life. How you choose to spend it is how you choose to live. Make those choices consciously, intentionally, and with purpose. Because in the end, a life well-lived is the ultimate measure of productivity.

Now, go forth and make every moment count. Your future self will thank you.

CHAPTER TEN

Financial Management for Entrepreneurs

As an entrepreneur, you're not just chasing a paycheck—you're pursuing a dream. You've taken the brave step of venturing out on your own, fueled by passion and a vision of what could be. But here's the truth that many starry-eyed founders don't want to face: even the most brilliant idea or innovative product won't save you if you can't manage your money.

I've been there. I've felt the exhilaration of landing that first big client, and the gut-wrenching panic of realizing I didn't have enough in the bank to make payroll. I've experienced sleepless nights staring at spreadsheets, wondering how I was going to keep the lights on for another month. And I've tasted the sweet victory of turning things around and building a thriving business that not only survives but thrives.

That's why I'm writing this section with every ounce of passion and hard-won wisdom I can muster. Because I know that mastering financial management isn't just about numbers—it's about giving your dreams a fighting chance. It's about creating a solid foundation that will allow your vision to soar. And most importantly, it's about empowering you to build something lasting and meaningful that can change lives—including your own.

So let's dive in, shall we? Buckle up, because we're about to embark on a journey that will transform the way you think about money in your business. And I promise you this: if you embrace these principles and put them into practice, you'll be amazed at what you can achieve.

The Mindset Shift: From Creator to CEO

The first and most crucial step in mastering financial management as an entrepreneur is a profound shift in mindset. You see, when most of us start our businesses, we're driven by our craft. We're the brilliant coder, the visionary designer, the innovative engineer. And that's beautiful—it's that passion that gives our ventures their spark.

But here's the hard truth: to succeed in the long run, you need to become more than just a creator. You need to step into the role of CEO. And a huge part of that role is becoming the financial steward of your business.

I remember the moment this reality hit me like a ton of bricks. I was six months into my first startup, burning through cash faster than I could bring it in. I was so focused on perfecting our product that I'd neglected the numbers. And suddenly, I realized that if I didn't get a handle on our finances, all of our hard work would be for nothing.

That night, I made a decision. I wasn't going to be just another passionate founder who flamed out because they couldn't manage money. I was going to learn everything I could about financial management, even if it meant stepping way out of my comfort zone.

And you know what? It was uncomfortable. It was frustrating. There were times I wanted to throw my laptop out the window and go back to doing what I loved. But I persevered, and that decision changed everything.

So, my fellow entrepreneur, I challenge you to make that

same commitment today. Embrace the role of CEO. Own your numbers. Because when you do, you're not just managing finances—you're taking control of your destiny.

Cash is King: Understanding and Managing Your Cash Flow

Now that you've committed to owning your financial future, let's talk about the lifeblood of your business: cash flow.

Imagine cash flow as the heartbeat of your company. Just as a strong, steady heartbeat is essential for a healthy body, a positive cash flow is crucial for a thriving business. But here's the kicker: profitability doesn't always equal positive cash flow. You can be turning a profit on paper and still find yourself unable to pay your bills.

I learned this lesson the hard way. In my second year of business, we landed a huge contract—the kind that had us popping champagne and dreaming of early retirement. But our client had 90-day payment terms, and we had to invest heavily upfront to deliver the project. Suddenly, we found ourselves in a cash crunch, scrambling to cover expenses while we waited for that big payday.

That experience taught me the importance of not just tracking cash flow, but actively managing it. Here are some strategies that have been game-changers for me and countless other entrepreneurs:

1. Create a cash flow forecast: This is your crystal ball, helping you predict and prepare for potential cash shortages. Update it regularly and use it to make informed decisions about spending and investments.

2. Negotiate favorable payment terms: With both clients and suppliers. The goal is to get paid as quickly as possible while extending your own payment terms where you can.

3. Build a cash reserve: Aim for at least three to six months of operating expenses. This buffer can be the difference between weathering a storm and closing your doors.

4. Consider alternative financing options: Lines of credit, invoice factoring, or even peer-to-peer lending can help bridge cash flow gaps.

Remember, cash flow management isn't just about survival—it's about creating the freedom to seize opportunities when they arise. When you have a healthy cash flow, you can invest in growth, take calculated risks, and sleep better at night knowing you're prepared for whatever comes your way.

The Power of Financial Forecasting: Charting Your Course to Success

Now that we've got a handle on cash flow, let's talk about one of the most powerful tools in your financial arsenal: forecasting. If cash flow is the heartbeat of your business, think of financial forecasting as your GPS, guiding you toward your destination and helping you navigate obstacles along the way.

I'll never forget the first time I created a truly comprehensive financial forecast for my business. It was like putting on glasses after years of squinting—suddenly, everything came into focus. I could see potential pitfalls months in advance, identify opportunities for growth, and make decisions with confidence.

But I'll be honest: creating that first forecast was daunting. I stared at the blank spreadsheet, feeling overwhelmed and unsure where to start. Maybe you're feeling that way right now. If so, take a deep breath. Remember, forecasting isn't about predicting the future with perfect accuracy—it's about creating a roadmap that will guide your decisions.

Start by projecting your revenue. Be realistic, but don't be afraid to dream big. Then, estimate your expenses—everything from salaries and rent to marketing costs and office supplies. Don't forget to factor in seasonality, market trends, and your growth plans.

Once you have your basic forecast, the real magic begins. Start playing with the numbers. What happens if you raise your prices by 10%? What if you invest in a new marketing campaign? What if a key client leaves? By running these scenarios, you're not just crunching numbers—you're rehearsing for different futures, preparing yourself to make swift, informed decisions when the time comes.

But here's the key: your forecast is a living document. Review and update it regularly. As you gain more data and experience, your projections will become more accurate, and your decision-making will improve.

Remember, financial forecasting isn't just about predicting numbers—it's about painting a picture of the future you want to create, and then figuring out how to make it a reality. It's about turning your entrepreneurial vision into a concrete plan of action. And when you do it right, it's nothing short of exhilarating.

Profit First: Rewriting the Rules of Business Finance

Now, let's talk about a concept that revolutionized the way I think about business finances: Profit First. This approach, popularized by Mike Michalowicz, turns traditional accounting on its head in a way that can be truly transformative for entrepreneurs.

Here's the conventional wisdom: Sales-Expenses = Profit. It seems logical, right? You make money, you pay your bills, and whatever's left over is your profit. But there's a big problem with this approach: too often, there's nothing left over. We end up treating profit as an afterthought, rather than a priority.

Profit First flips the script. The new formula becomes: Sales-Profit = Expenses. In other words, you take your profit first and then figure out how to run your business on what's left. It sounds simple, but the psychological impact is profound.

When I first implemented Profit First in my business, it felt uncomfortable, even a little scary. How could I possibly make a profit when there were so many expenses to cover? But I committed to the process, starting small with just 1% profit. And you know what? It changed everything.

Suddenly, profit wasn't this elusive goal always just out of reach. It was a real, tangible thing that existed in my business from day one. It forced me to get creative about cutting costs and increasing efficiency. Most importantly, it shifted my mindset from constantly chasing growth to focusing on building a sustainably profitable business.

Here's how you can start implementing Profit First today:

1. Set up separate bank accounts for Revenue, Profit, Owner's Pay, Taxes, and Operating Expenses.

2. Determine your Target Allocation Percentages for each account based on your current revenue.

3. Every time you receive payment, immediately distribute

the money into these accounts according to your percentages.

4. Only pay expenses out of your Operating Expenses account.

5. Take your profit distribution quarterly—this is your reward for building a profitable business!

Now, I won't sugarcoat it: implementing Profit First can be challenging, especially if you're used to operating close to the edge financially. But stick with it. Start small if you need to, even with just 1% profit. As you see that profit account growing, I promise you'll be motivated to find ways to increase it.

Remember, the goal isn't just to make money—it's to build a business that serves your life, not the other way around. Profit First helps ensure that your hard work translates into real financial rewards, not just an endless cycle of covering expenses.

The Art of Financial Storytelling: Making Your Numbers Come Alive

As we dive deeper into financial management, I want to touch on a skill that's often overlooked but incredibly powerful: financial storytelling. Because here's the truth—numbers alone don't inspire people. Stories do.

Think about it. When you're pitching to investors, negotiating with suppliers, or rallying your team, you're not just presenting data—you're telling the story of your business. And your financials are a crucial part of that story.

I learned the power of financial storytelling early in my entrepreneurial journey. I was seeking investment for my startup, and my first pitch was a disaster. I bombarded the investors with charts, graphs, and spreadsheets, thinking I was impressing them with my thoroughness. Instead, their eyes glazed over, and I lost them completely.

Determined to do better, I completely revamped my approach for the next pitch. Instead of just presenting numbers, I wove them into a compelling narrative. I showed how each figure represented a milestone in our journey, a challenge overcome, or an opportunity seized. I painted a vivid picture of where we were heading and how their investment would fuel our growth.

The difference was night and day. The investors were engaged, asking questions, and genuinely excited about our vision. We walked out of that meeting with a term sheet in hand.

So how can you become a master of financial storytelling? Here are some tips:

1. Know your audience: Tailor your story to what matters most to them. An investor cares about different things than a team member or a customer.

2. Use visuals wisely: Don't overwhelm with data. Choose key metrics that illustrate your points and present them in a clear, visually appealing way.

3. Provide context: Don't just state numbers—explain what they mean. How do they compare to industry standards? What trends do they reveal?

4. Highlight the human element: Remember, behind every number is a person—a customer served, an employee supported, a community impacted.

5. Practice, practice, practice: The more comfortable you are with your numbers, the more naturally you'll be able to weave them into your story.

Financial storytelling isn't about manipulating or embellishing—it's about bringing your numbers to life in a way that resonates with your audience. It's about showing how the cold, hard figures translate into real-world impact and opportunity.

Master this skill, and you'll find doors opening that you never thought possible. You'll inspire confidence in investors, alignment in your team, and trust in your customers. Because when you can tell a compelling financial story, you're not just sharing numbers—you're sharing your vision for the future.

Embracing Financial Technology: Your Secret Weapon for Success

As we near the end of our journey through financial management, I want to touch on a topic that has the power to completely transform the way you handle your business finances: technology.

When I started my first business, financial management was a nightmare of spreadsheets, paper receipts, and late nights hunched over a calculator. I spent so much time buried in administrative tasks that I had little energy left for actually growing my business. Sound familiar?

But then I discovered the world of financial technology, or "fintech," and it was like stepping into the future. Suddenly, tasks that used to take hours could be done in minutes. Data that was once scattered across multiple systems was now integrated and accessible at the click of a button. It was nothing short of revolutionary.

Today, there's an incredible array of tools available to help entrepreneurs manage their finances more efficiently and effectively. From cloud-based accounting software to AI-powered forecasting tools, the options can seem overwhelming. But trust me, investing the time to find and implement the right tech stack for your business is one of the best decisions you can make.

Here are some areas where fintech can make a huge difference:

1. Accounting and Bookkeeping: Tools like QuickBooks Online or Xero can automate much of your bookkeeping, saving time and reducing errors.

2. Invoicing and Payments: Platforms like Stripe or Square can streamline your payment processes, improving cash flow and providing valuable data.

3. Expense Management: Apps like Expensify or Rydoo can make tracking and categorizing expenses a breeze.

4. Financial Planning and Analysis: Tools like Adaptive Insights or Anaplan can take your forecasting and budgeting to the next level.

5. Cash Flow Management: Platforms like Float or Pulse can give you real-time visibility into your cash position and help you plan for the future.

But here's the key: technology is a tool, not a solution in itself. The real power comes from how you use it. Take the time to properly set up and learn your chosen tools. Integrate them into your daily operations. Use the insights they provide to make better decisions.

And remember, the goal of embracing fintech isn't just to save time (although that's a wonderful benefit). It's about gaining deeper insights into your business, making more informed decisions, and ultimately, driving growth and profitability.

As you explore the world of financial technology, stay curious and open-minded. The landscape is constantly evolving, with new tools and capabilities emerging all the time. What seems cutting-edge today may be standard practice tomorrow. By staying ahead of the curve, you're not just managing your finances more effectively—you're gaining a competitive edge in your industry.

The Journey Continues: Your Financial Evolution as an Entrepreneur

As we wrap up this exploration of financial management for entrepreneurs, I want to leave you with one final thought: this journey never truly ends. As your business grows and evolves, so too will your financial needs and challenges.

The strategies and tools that serve you well today may need to be refined or replaced as you scale. The financial decisions that seem daunting now will become second nature, only to be replaced by new, more complex challenges. And that's okay—in fact, it's something to be embraced.

Because here's the beautiful truth about entrepreneurship: it's a path of constant growth and learning. Every financial hurdle you overcome, and every new skill you master, makes you stronger and more capable as a business leader.

Remember that nervous founder I described at the beginning, staring at a blank spreadsheet and feeling overwhelmed? That was me, not so long ago. Now, I navigate complex financial decisions with confidence, use advanced forecasting tools to plan for the future, and have built a business with a healthy, sustainable profit margin.

But I'm not special or uniquely gifted. I simply committed to the journey of financial mastery, one step at a time. And you can do the same.

So here's my challenge to you: embrace your role as the financial steward of your business. Commit to continuous learning and improvement. Stay curious, stay hungry, and never stop pushing yourself to new levels of financial acumen.

Start with the basics we've covered—understanding cash flow, creating forecasts, and implementing Profit First. As you master these, push yourself further. Dive into more advanced topics like financial modeling or risk management. Explore emerging technologies that can give you an edge.

And through it all, remember why you're doing this. It's not about the numbers for their own sake. It's about creating a business that not only survives but thrives. It's about building something that can weather any storm and seize every opportunity. It's about turning your entrepreneurial vision into a lasting reality that creates value for you, your team, your customers, and your community.

Financial management might not be why you became an entrepreneur. But mastering it can be what allows you to fulfill your entrepreneurial dreams. It's the foundation that will support every bold move, every innovation, every expansion.

So embrace this journey. Celebrate every small win along the way. And know that with each step you take towards financial mastery, you're not just improving your business—you're transforming yourself into the leader your vision deserves.

The road ahead may not always be easy, but I promise you, it's worth it. Because on the other side of the challenges and the learning curves lies the freedom and impact you've always dreamed of. And armed with the financial skills and mindset we've explored, you're ready to claim it.

Here's to your success, your growth, and the incredible journey ahead. The world is waiting for what you'll build. Now go out there and make it happen!

CHAPTER ELEVEN

Leadership and Building Effective Team

As I sit here, reflecting on my journey from a high school dropout to a successful real estate broker and business owner, I'm struck by how much of my success has been shaped by the people around me. Leadership isn't just about being at the top of the ladder; it's about lifting others up as you climb. Building a team isn't just about hiring people; it's about creating a family bound by shared goals and mutual respect. Let me take you on a journey through the highs and lows of leadership and team building, sharing the lessons I've learned along the way.

I remember the day I decided to start my own brokerage like it was yesterday. The excitement coursing through my veins was palpable, but so was the fear. I had been a successful agent, sure, but leading a team? That was a whole new ballgame. As I stood in the empty office space that would soon become Bliss Home Realty and Relocation Group, I felt the weight of responsibility settle on my shoulders. It wasn't just about me anymore; it was about the lives and careers of the people who would trust me to lead them.

The first few months were a whirlwind. I started with just one agent working alongside me, but I had big dreams. I wanted to create something special, a place where agents could thrive and grow. But let me tell you, those early days were tough. There were nights when I lay awake, wondering if I had made the right decision. The doubts would creep in, whispering that maybe I wasn't cut out for this leadership thing.

But then I'd remember where I came from. I'd think about

that kid from New Bedford who dropped out of high school and moved to New York City with just $35 in his pocket. If that kid could make it, then surely I could build a successful brokerage. It was that fire in my belly, that unwavering belief in myself and my vision, that got me through those challenging times.

As we started to grow, adding more agents to our team, I realized that leadership isn't about having all the answers. It's about creating an environment where people feel safe to ask questions, to make mistakes, and to learn. I made it a point to be approachable, and to have an open-door policy where any of my agents could come to me with their concerns or ideas.

I remember one particular day when a new agent, Sarah, came into my office. She was on the verge of tears, feeling overwhelmed and ready to quit. Instead of dismissing her concerns or giving her a pep talk, I sat her down and really listened. We talked for hours, not just about real estate, but about life, dreams, and fears. By the end of our conversation, Sarah didn't just feel better – she felt empowered. She went on to become one of our top-performing agents, and to this day, she credits that conversation as the turning point in her career.

That experience taught me a valuable lesson about leadership: it's not just about motivating people to work harder; it's about inspiring them to believe in themselves. As leaders, we have the power to shape the self-perception of our team members. A word of encouragement, a show of faith in their abilities, can be the catalyst that transforms a struggling agent into a superstar.

But leadership isn't always smooth sailing. There have been times when I've had to make tough decisions, like letting go of team members who weren't a good fit. Those moments are heart-wrenching, but they're necessary for the health of the team and the business. I've learned that being a good leader sometimes means being the bad guy, and making unpopular decisions for the greater good.

I remember having to let go of Mark, an agent who had been with us from the early days. He was a great guy, but his performance had been slipping for months, and he wasn't taking the steps to improve despite numerous conversations. The day I had to sit him down and tell him it wasn't working out was one of the hardest days of my career. I saw the disappointment in his eyes and felt the weight of his family's livelihood on my shoulders. But I knew that keeping him on would be a disservice to him, to the team, and to our clients.

That experience taught me the importance of clear communication and setting expectations from the start. Now, I make sure every team member knows exactly what's expected of them, and we have regular check-ins to address any issues before they become major problems. It's not always comfortable, but it's necessary for the growth and success of both the individual and the team.

Building a strong team isn't just about hiring the right people; it's about creating a culture where everyone feels valued and motivated to give their best. I've found that one of the most powerful ways to do this is by leading by example. I never ask my team to do something I wouldn't do myself. If we're having a late night preparing for a big listing presentation, I'm right there with them, ordering pizza and burning the midnight oil.

This approach has fostered a sense of camaraderie and mutual respect within our team. We're not just colleagues; we're a family. We celebrate each other's successes and support each other through the tough times. I remember when one of our agents, Tom, lost his mother unexpectedly. The entire team rallied around him, covering his listings, checking in on him, and even cooking meals for his family. That's the kind of culture I've always dreamed of creating – one where we're not just in it for the commissions, but for each other.

One of the most rewarding aspects of leadership is watching your team members grow and succeed. I take immense pride in nurturing talent and helping my agents reach their full potential. We have a comprehensive training program that goes beyond just teaching real estate skills. We focus on personal development, goal setting, and mindset training.

I believe that success in real estate – and in life – is 90% mindset and 10% skillset. You can teach someone the technical aspects of real estate, but if they don't believe in themselves, if they don't have the right mindset, they'll never reach their full potential. That's why I invest so much time and energy into helping my team develop a growth mindset.

We have weekly team meetings where we not only discuss business but also share personal goals and challenges. I encourage my team to dream big and to verbalize those dreams. There's power in speaking your goals out loud, in front of people who support you. I've seen agents who came to us with no experience transform into confident, successful professionals simply because they were in an environment that believed in them.

But leadership isn't just about the big, inspirational moments. It's about the small, everyday actions that show your team you care. It's about remembering birthdays, asking about their families, and celebrating their small wins. It's about being there when they need you, whether it's for a quick question about a contract or a shoulder to cry on after a tough day.

I make it a point to have one-on-one meetings with each of my agents regularly. These aren't just about reviewing numbers or discussing targets. They're about connecting on a human level, understanding their aspirations, their fears, and their challenges. I share my own experiences, my own failures, and how I overcame them. This vulnerability creates a bond of trust that goes beyond the typical boss-employee relationship.

One of the most important lessons I've learned about leadership is the power of empowerment. As the leader, it's tempting to want to control everything, to be involved in every decision. But true leadership is about giving your team the tools, the knowledge, and the confidence to make decisions on their own.

I remember when I first started delegating important tasks to my team. It was terrifying. What if they made a mistake? What if they didn't do it the way I would? But I quickly realized that by holding on too tightly, I was stunting their growth and limiting the potential of the business.

Now, I focus on clearly communicating our vision and values, and then I step back and let my team run with it. Sure, there are mistakes sometimes, but we treat those as learning opportunities, not failures. This approach has not only helped our team members grow but has also allowed the business to scale in ways I never thought possible.

Building a strong team also means fostering a culture of continuous learning and improvement. In the fast-paced world of real estate, staying stagnant is not an option. We need to be constantly evolving, learning new skills, and adapting to changes in the market.

To this end, we have a robust system of ongoing education and training. We bring in experts for workshops, send our agents to conferences, and encourage them to pursue additional certifications. But more than that, we foster a culture where asking questions and seeking help is encouraged.

I often tell my team, "The only stupid question is the one you don't ask." I want them to feel comfortable coming to me or their colleagues when they're unsure about something. This open exchange of knowledge and ideas has been crucial to our success.

One of the most challenging aspects of leadership is managing different personalities and working styles. In any team, you'll have a mix of introverts and extroverts, detail-oriented people and big-picture thinkers, risk-takers and cautious planners. The key is to recognize these differences and leverage them for the benefit of the team.

I've learned to tailor my leadership style to each individual. For some, a gentle word of encouragement is all they need to thrive. For others, a more direct approach works better. It's about understanding what motivates each person and creating an environment where they can play to their strengths.

This individualized approach extends to how we structure our teams for different projects. When we're working on a big listing presentation, I make sure to include both the creative thinkers who can come up with innovative marketing ideas and the detail-oriented folks who will ensure every number in the CMA is spot-on.

Another crucial aspect of leadership is transparency. I believe in being open and honest with my team, even when the news isn't good. When the market took a downturn a few years ago, I called a team meeting. I laid out the challenges we were facing, but I also shared my vision for how we were going to not just survive but thrive in the new reality.

This transparency builds trust and fosters a sense of ownership among the team. They're not just along for the ride; they're active participants in shaping the future of the business. It's amazing to see how people step up when they feel truly invested in the outcome.

One of the most rewarding aspects of leadership is seeing your team members achieve things they never thought possible. I remember Lisa, an agent who joined us fresh out of real estate school. She was shy, unsure of herself, and terrified of cold calling. But she had a passion for real estate and a willingness to learn.

We worked together closely, role-playing scenarios, practicing scripts, and gradually building her confidence. I still remember the day she closed her first million-dollar listing. The look of pride and accomplishment on her face was priceless. Moments like these remind me why I do what I do. It's not just about the deals or the money; it's about helping people realize their potential and achieve their dreams.

Building a strong team also means creating a supportive environment where it's okay to fail. In real estate, not every deal is going to close, not every listing presentation is going to be a success. What matters is how we respond to these setbacks.

I encourage my team to view failures as learning opportunities. Whenever we lose a deal, we do a post-mortem analysis. What could we have done differently? What can we learn from this experience? This approach takes the sting out of failure and turns it into a stepping stone for future success.

One of the most important lessons I've learned about leadership is the power of recognition and appreciation. People want to feel valued for their contributions. It's not just about monetary rewards, although those are important too. It's about acknowledging their hard work, their creativity, their dedication.

We have a weekly "shout-out" session where team members can recognize each other for going above and beyond. It could be for closing a big deal, helping a colleague with a difficult client, or even something as simple as bringing in coffee for everyone on a busy morning. These moments of recognition create a positive atmosphere and reinforce the behaviors we want to see more of.

As our team has grown, maintaining our culture has become both more challenging and more important. It's easy to have a tight-knit culture when you're a small team of five or ten people. But how do you maintain that family feeling when you're fifty or a hundred strong?

The key, I've found, is to be intentional about it. We have regular team-building activities, both in and out of the office. We volunteer together in the community, have family picnics, and celebrate milestones together. These shared experiences create bonds that go beyond the workplace.

We also have a mentorship program where experienced agents take newcomers under their wing. This not only helps the new agents get up to speed faster but also reinforces our culture of collaboration and mutual support.

Looking back on my journey as a leader, I'm filled with a sense of pride and gratitude. Pride in what we've built together as a team, and gratitude for the trust my team members have placed in me. But I also feel a sense of responsibility – to continue growing, learning, and being the best leader I can be for my team.

Leadership isn't a destination; it's a journey. Every day brings new challenges, and new opportunities to learn and grow. I'm not perfect – far from it. I've made mistakes, I've had moments of doubt, I've faced challenges that seemed insurmountable. But through it all, I've learned that true leadership isn't about being infallible. It's about being authentic, being willing to learn, and always putting your team first.

To those of you reading this who aspire to leadership roles, I want to leave you with this thought: Leadership isn't about titles or corner offices. It's about impact. It's about making a positive difference in the lives of those you lead. It's about creating an environment where people can grow, thrive, and achieve their dreams.

Remember, you don't need to have it all figured out to be a leader. You just need to have a vision, the courage to pursue it, and the humility to bring others along on the journey. Leadership is a privilege, a responsibility, and an incredible opportunity to shape not just a business, but people's lives.

As you embark on your own leadership journey, be patient with yourself. Learn from your mistakes. Celebrate your successes, no matter how small. And above all, never forget the power you have to inspire, motivate, and uplift those around you.

Building a strong team and being an effective leader isn't always easy. There will be days when you question yourself, when the challenges seem overwhelming. But I promise you, it's worth it. The satisfaction of seeing your team succeed, of knowing you played a part in someone achieving their dreams – there's nothing quite like it.

So go forth with courage, with compassion, and with the unwavering belief that you can make a difference. Because you can. You have within you the power to be not just a boss, but a true leader – someone who inspires, who uplifts, who brings out the best in others.

And remember, leadership isn't about being perfect. It's about being present, being authentic, and always striving to be better. It's about creating a vision so compelling that others want to be part of it. It's about building not just a team, but a community – a place where people feel valued, supported, and inspired to give their best.

As you face the challenges and joys of leadership, always keep your why at the forefront. Why did you choose this path? What difference do you want to make in the world? Let that purpose guide you, sustain you, and inspire you to keep pushing forward, even when the going gets tough.

In the end, your legacy as a leader won't be measured in deals closed or profits made. It will be measured in the lives you've touched, the careers you've launched, and the dreams you've helped realize. That's the true measure of success in leadership.

So here's to you, future leaders. May you lead with courage, with compassion, and with an unwavering commitment to bringing out the best in others. The world needs more leaders like you – leaders who understand that true success comes not from climbing over others, but from lifting others as you climb.

Remember, every great journey begins with a single step. Your journey to becoming a great leader starts now. Embrace it, learn from it, and most importantly, enjoy it. The road ahead may not always be easy, but I promise you, it will be worth it. Here's to your success, to your growth, and to the incredible impact you're going to make as a leader. The world is waiting for you. Go out there and make your mark!

CHAPTER TWELVE

The Power of Mindset

The human mind is an incredibly powerful tool, capable of shaping our reality and determining our destiny. One of the most transformative concepts in psychology is the idea of a growth mindset, a term popularized by Dr. Carol Dweck. A growth mindset is the belief that our abilities, intelligence, and talents can be developed through dedication, hard work, and learning. This mindset contrasts sharply with a fixed mindset, where individuals believe their qualities are static and unchangeable. Embracing a growth mindset can profoundly impact every aspect of our lives, enabling us to overcome obstacles, achieve our goals, and realize our full potential.

This kind of "I can get better," "I can do better," and "There is a better way to this," is one of the major pathways to success. There is no one who sabotages themselves whoever gets successful, if they do, it is by chance. As you read this book, let it be very strong in your mind that you can actually get better with anything you do. If you believe that you can grow, then you'll have it. You cannot grow beyond what you have in your mind.

Developing a growth mindset begins with how we perceive challenges. Challenges are an inevitable part of life. They can be intimidating and overwhelming, often leading us to doubt our abilities. However, with a growth mindset, challenges are seen not as threats but as opportunities for growth and learning. This shift in perspective can make a world of difference.

I remember when I moved to New York City with just $35

in my pocket. At the time, it felt like the most daunting challenge I had ever faced. I had no safety net, no connections, and no clear plan. The city was overwhelming, and there were days when I doubted whether I had made the right decision. However, I embraced the challenge, viewing it as an opportunity to learn and grow. I took on any job I could find, from handing out flyers on street corners to cold-calling for the New York Post. Each experience taught me valuable lessons about resilience, adaptability, and the importance of hard work. Over time, these lessons helped me build a foundation for my future success.

Similarly, learning from failure is a critical component of a growth mindset. Failure is often perceived as a negative experience, something to be avoided at all costs. However, from a growth mindset perspective, failure is not the end but a crucial part of the learning process. It provides invaluable lessons and opportunities for improvement.

Before achieving success in real estate, I faced numerous setbacks and rejections. One of the most memorable was when I applied for a position at a real estate company in New York and was turned down because I lacked experience. Instead of letting this rejection defeat me, I used it as motivation to gain the experience I needed. I worked alongside my partner, who had been hired by the company, helping him with research and client interactions. This behind-the-scenes involvement allowed me to learn the ropes and build my skills. When the time was right, I was ready to step into the industry with confidence. My journey highlights the importance of viewing failure as feedback rather than a final verdict.

Effort is another cornerstone of developing a growth mindset. In a world that often celebrates instant success and natural talent, it can be easy to overlook the value of hard work and effort. A growth mindset, however, emphasizes the importance of effort in achieving mastery. It is through sustained effort and practice that we develop our skills and abilities. This perspective encourages us to take pride in our efforts and see them as essential components of our growth and development.

In my own life, I have always believed in giving 110% to everything I do. Even on days when I felt like staying in bed or spending time with my son, I chose to get up and hustle. This relentless dedication has been a key factor in my success. For instance, when I worked as an assistant manager at McDonald's, I didn't just do my job; I went above and beyond, learning everything I could about leadership and business operations. This dedication eventually led to my promotion to general manager, where I managed up to 70 employees. By adopting a similar mindset, we can strive for excellence in our own endeavors, recognizing that effort is the key to unlocking our full potential.

The ability to accept and learn from criticism is also vital in fostering a growth mindset. Criticism can be difficult to hear, especially when it feels personal or unjust. However, constructive criticism is a powerful tool for growth and improvement. A growth mindset encourages us to view criticism as feedback that can help us identify areas for development and enhance our performance. Instead of taking criticism personally, we can use it as a valuable resource to guide our progress.

Early in my career, I faced significant criticism. I was told that I was unfit for certain roles and even fired from jobs. Rather than letting these critiques diminish my self-worth, I used them as fuel to refine my skills and prove my detractors wrong. For example, after being told I wasn't ready for a real estate career, I worked harder to gain the necessary experience and knowledge. This persistence paid off when I eventually secured my real estate license and began building a successful career. My ability to learn from criticism and continually improve myself has been a crucial factor in my journey.

Finding inspiration in others' success is another way to cultivate a growth mindset. In a competitive world, it is easy to view others' success with envy or resentment. However, a growth mindset encourages us to find lessons and inspiration in the achievements of others. By understanding the hard work, dedication, and strategies that contributed to their success, we can gain valuable insights that can be applied to our own journeys.

Throughout my career, I have looked up to successful individuals in my industry, learning from their stories and strategies. One such example is a mentor who guided me through the complexities of real estate investing. Their success and willingness to share their knowledge inspired me to push harder and aim higher. By finding role models and learning from their experiences, we can accelerate our own growth and achieve our goals more effectively.

To truly develop a growth mindset, we must also cultivate a love for learning. This involves being curious, open-minded, and willing to explore new ideas and perspectives. It means being committed to lifelong learning and recognizing that there is always more to learn. This attitude can transform our approach to both personal and professional development, opening up new avenues for growth and achievement. When we see ourselves as perpetual learners, we are more likely to take risks, embrace challenges, and persist in the face of setbacks.

The journey to developing a growth mindset is ongoing and requires conscious effort. It involves reprogramming our thought patterns, challenging our assumptions, and being willing to step out of our comfort zones. It is about embracing the process of growth and understanding that progress often comes in small, incremental steps rather than giant leaps. By committing to this journey, we can unlock our true potential and achieve things we once thought impossible.

Developing a growth mindset is a powerful way to transform our lives. It enables us to embrace challenges, learn from failure, value effort, accept criticism, find inspiration in others, and cultivate a love for learning. By adopting a growth mindset, we can overcome obstacles, achieve our goals, and realize our full potential. This mindset not only enhances our personal and professional lives but also inspires those around us to strive for greatness. In the end, the power of mindset is a testament to the boundless possibilities that lie within each of us, waiting to be unleashed.

CHAPTER THIRTEEN

Overcoming Self-Doubt and Limiting Beliefs

Self-doubt and limiting beliefs are among the most formidable barriers to personal and professional growth. It is very unlikely that you'll navigate life without some elements of self-doubts. The good news is that self-doubt is part of the process. Chimamanda Ngozi Adichie, one of the global giants in literature once said:

"You cannot create anything of value without both self-doubt and self-belief. Without self-doubt, you become complacent; without self-belief, you cannot succeed."

Self-doubts are negative thoughts that are not necessarily bad in themselves. What is bad is how we decide to take advantage of them.

These negative thoughts and feelings can hinder us from pursuing our dreams, achieving our goals, and realizing our full potential. However, overcoming self-doubt and limiting beliefs is possible with the right mindset, strategies, and support. This journey requires introspection, perseverance, and a commitment to personal development, but the rewards are immense. By breaking free from these mental chains, we can unlock our true potential and lead more fulfilling lives.

I remember vividly the times when self-doubt and limiting beliefs threatened to derail my aspirations. When I first decided to pursue a career in real estate, I was plagued with thoughts of inadequacy. Coming from a background of poverty and having dropped out of high school, I constantly questioned whether I had what it took to succeed in such a competitive field. My inner critic was relentless, reminding me of every failure and every reason why I might not succeed.

The first step in overcoming self-doubt is *recognizing and acknowledging it.* Self-doubt often manifests as a voice in our heads, telling us we are not good enough or that we don't deserve success. It's crucial to identify this voice and understand that it is not an accurate reflection of our abilities or potential. Instead, it is a learned response to past experiences and societal conditioning. By acknowledging its presence, we can begin to challenge and change these negative thought patterns.

One technique that helped me was reframing my self-doubt into questions and positive affirmations. Instead of thinking, *"I can't do this,"* I would ask myself, *"What steps can I take to improve my skills and knowledge to succeed in this task?"* This shift in perspective transformed my self-doubt into a problem-solving mindset, empowering me to take action rather than be paralyzed by fear.

Limiting beliefs are closely related to self-doubt. These are deeply ingrained convictions that restrict our thinking and behavior. They often stem from childhood experiences, cultural norms, or past failures. For instance, I grew up believing that success was only attainable for those with a formal education and a privileged background. This belief limited my aspirations and made me hesitant to pursue ambitious goals.

To overcome limiting beliefs, we must first identify them. This requires introspection and honest reflection. Writing down our beliefs and examining their origins can be enlightening. Once we have identified our limiting beliefs, we can challenge their validity. Are these beliefs based on facts or assumptions? Are there examples of people who have succeeded despite similar challenges? By questioning the validity of our limiting beliefs, we can begin to dismantle them.

One powerful method to counteract limiting beliefs is to *surround ourselves with positive influences.* Mentors, role models, and supportive friends can provide encouragement and perspective. When I was starting out in real estate, I sought out mentors who had overcome similar obstacles. Their stories of perseverance and success inspired me and provided valuable insights. These mentors helped me see that my limiting beliefs were not insurmountable barriers but challenges that could be overcome with determination and hard work.

Another crucial aspect of overcoming self-doubt and limiting beliefs is *setting realistic and achievable goals.* Large, long-term goals can be daunting and may exacerbate self-doubt. Breaking these goals down into smaller, manageable steps can make them more attainable and reduce feelings of overwhelm. Each small success builds confidence and reinforces the belief that we are capable of achieving our larger aspirations.

When I decided to get my real estate license, I broke the process down into manageable steps: studying for the exam, passing the exam, finding a brokerage, and so on. Celebrating each milestone, no matter how small, helped me build momentum and confidence. This approach not only made the goal seem less daunting but also provided a clear path forward.

Mindfulness and self-compassion are also essential tools in overcoming self-doubt. Mindfulness involves being present and fully engaged in the current moment, without judgment. It helps us become aware of our negative thoughts and emotions without being consumed by them. Self-compassion involves treating ourselves with kindness and understanding, especially in the face of failure or difficulty. By practicing mindfulness and self-compassion, we can develop a healthier relationship with ourselves and reduce the power of self-doubt.

I recall a time when a major real estate deal fell through. I was devastated and began to doubt my abilities. However, instead of berating myself, I practiced self-compassion. I acknowledged that setbacks are a natural part of the learning process and reminded myself of my past successes. This compassionate approach helped me bounce back more quickly and maintain my confidence.

Visualization is another powerful technique for overcoming self-doubt and limiting beliefs. Visualizing success and vividly imagining ourselves achieving our goals can reinforce positive beliefs and reduce anxiety. When we repeatedly visualize ourselves succeeding, our brain begins to associate these positive images with reality, making us more likely to take the necessary actions to achieve our goals.

Before important meetings or presentations, I often visualize myself performing confidently and successfully. This practice helps me calm my nerves and approach the situation with a positive mindset. Visualization has been a crucial tool in building my self-confidence and overcoming self-doubt.

Finally, seeking professional help can be beneficial. Therapists, coaches, and counselors can provide strategies and support to help us overcome self-doubt and limiting beliefs. They can offer a different perspective and help us develop personalized action plans to address our specific challenges.

Overcoming self-doubt and limiting beliefs is a transformative process that requires self-awareness, perseverance, and support. By recognizing and challenging our negative thoughts, reframing our perspective, surrounding ourselves with positive influences, setting realistic goals, practicing mindfulness and self-compassion, using visualization techniques, and seeking professional help, we can break free from the mental chains that hold us back. As we embark on this journey, we unlock our true potential and open the door to a world of possibilities. The path may be challenging, but the rewards are well worth the effort. Embrace the journey, and believe in your ability to overcome any obstacle that comes your way.

The importance of visualization and goal-setting

What do you see now? What are you looking out for? Hey... No, I'm not talking about what you see physically. I'm talking about what you see in your mind. In the pursuit of personal and professional success, the practices of visualization and goal-setting stand out as fundamental tools. These techniques not only help us clarify our aspirations but also provide a roadmap to achieve them. Visualization and goal-setting are closely linked, as visualizing our goals can make them feel more tangible and attainable. By harnessing the power of these practices, we can transform our dreams into reality and navigate the path to success with confidence and clarity.

Visualization is the practice of creating vivid mental images of desired outcomes. This technique taps into the power of the mind to influence our actions and emotions. When we visualize success, we engage our brain in a way that enhances motivation, reduces anxiety, and increases the likelihood of achieving our goals. This mental rehearsal prepares us for real-life situations, making us more confident and effective in our pursuits.

I vividly remember the first time I used visualization to overcome a significant challenge. Early in my real estate career, I had a crucial presentation that could make or break a major deal. I was filled with anxiety and self-doubt, unsure of my ability to succeed. To combat these feelings, I began to visualize myself confidently presenting my proposal, answering questions with ease, and ultimately closing the deal. I repeated this mental rehearsal several times, vividly imagining every detail of the successful outcome. When the day of the presentation arrived, I felt prepared and composed. My visualization had transformed my anxiety into confidence, and I delivered the presentation flawlessly, securing the deal.

Visualization not only helps us prepare for specific events but also reinforces our belief in our ability to achieve our goals. By consistently imagining our success, we create a mental blueprint that guides our actions and decisions. This process aligns our subconscious mind with our conscious goals, making it easier to stay focused and motivated.

Goal-setting, on the other hand, is the process of defining clear, specific, and achievable objectives. Goals provide direction and purpose, helping us prioritize our efforts and measure our progress. Without goals, we risk drifting aimlessly, unsure of where to direct our energy and resources. Setting goals gives us a sense of purpose and a clear target to strive for.

When I decided to transition from my initial jobs to a career in real estate, I knew I needed a clear plan. I started by setting specific goals: obtaining my real estate license, securing my first clients, and eventually establishing my own brokerage. These goals were not vague aspirations but concrete, measurable targets. Breaking them down into smaller, manageable steps made the path to success seem less daunting and more attainable. For instance, to obtain my real estate license, I set a schedule for studying, enrolled in courses, and planned my exam dates. Each small achievement brought me closer to my ultimate goal, providing a sense of accomplishment and motivation to keep going.

One of the most effective ways to set goals is by using the SMART criteria—Specific, Measurable, Achievable, Relevant, and Time-bound. This framework ensures that our goals are clear and actionable. For example, instead of setting a vague goal like "I want to be successful in real estate," a SMART goal would be "I will obtain my real estate license within six months and secure my first three clients within the first year." This goal is specific (obtaining a license and securing clients), measurable (three clients), achievable (within the realm of possibility), relevant (aligned with my career aspirations), and time-bound (six months and one year).

Combining visualization with goal-setting creates a powerful synergy. Visualization helps us see the end result, while goal-setting outlines the steps to get there. This combination keeps us motivated and focused, even when faced with obstacles and setbacks. When we visualize our goals, we create a compelling image of our desired future, which serves as a constant reminder of why we are working hard and what we are striving to achieve.

Throughout my journey, I have encountered numerous challenges that tested my resolve. There were times when the path seemed unclear and the obstacles insurmountable. During these moments, visualization and goal-setting were my anchors. By revisiting my goals and visualizing my success, I could regain my focus and push through difficulties. One particularly challenging period was when I faced multiple rejections from potential clients. Instead of succumbing to self-doubt, I visualized myself successfully closing deals and growing my client base. I reviewed my goals, adjusted my strategies, and kept moving forward. This persistence paid off, as I eventually secured the clients I needed and built a thriving business.

Visualization and goal-setting also foster resilience. When we encounter setbacks, having clear goals and a vivid vision of success can help us stay motivated and persevere. They remind us of our purpose and the potential rewards of our efforts. This resilience is crucial, as the journey to success is rarely straightforward. It involves overcoming obstacles, learning from failures, and continuously adapting to new challenges.

In my experience, one of the most rewarding aspects of visualization and goal-setting is the sense of empowerment they provide. Knowing that I have a clear plan and the ability to envision my success gives me the confidence to take bold actions and pursue ambitious goals. This empowerment is not limited to professional achievements but extends to all areas of life. Whether it's personal growth, relationships, or health, visualization, and goal-setting can help us create a fulfilling and balanced life.

The importance of visualization and goal-setting cannot be overstated. These practices are essential tools for achieving success and realizing our full potential. Visualization helps us mentally prepare for challenges and reinforces our belief in our abilities, while goal-setting provides direction and a roadmap to success. Together, they create a powerful framework for personal and professional growth.

By embracing these techniques, we can overcome obstacles, stay motivated, and transform our dreams into reality. The journey may be challenging, but with visualization and goal-setting, we have the tools to navigate it with confidence and clarity.

CHAPTER FOURTEEN

Overcoming Adversity

Dealing with Rejection and Setbacks

Life is full of challenges, and everyone experiences rejection and setbacks at some point. Whether it's a missed opportunity, a failed project, or a personal disappointment, these experiences can be disheartening and difficult to navigate. However, how we respond to rejection and setbacks is what truly defines our ability to overcome adversity. Developing resilience and a positive mindset is essential for bouncing back and continuing on the path to success.

Rejection and setbacks are inevitable, but they do not define our worth or potential. Early in my career, I faced numerous rejections. One of the most memorable was when I applied for a position at a prestigious real estate firm in New York City. I had poured my heart and soul into the application process, confident that I was the perfect candidate. When I received the rejection letter, it felt like a punch to the gut. I questioned my abilities and wondered if I would ever succeed in the competitive real estate market.

The first step in dealing with rejection is to ***acknowledge your feelings.*** It's natural to feel disappointed, frustrated, and even angry when things don't go as planned. Allow yourself to experience these emotions, but don't let them consume you. Give yourself time to process the setback, and then shift your focus to what you can learn from the experience. Every rejection is an opportunity to gain insights and grow stronger.

In my case, after the initial disappointment subsided, I reflected on the feedback I had received during the application process. I realized there were areas where I could improve, such as my knowledge of certain real estate markets and my presentation skills. Instead of dwelling on the rejection, I decided to use it as a learning experience. I enrolled in courses to enhance my market knowledge and sought mentorship to refine my skills. This proactive approach not only improved my abilities but also boosted my confidence for future opportunities.

Another crucial aspect of overcoming rejection and setbacks is to **maintain a positive mindset.** It's easy to fall into a negative spiral when faced with adversity, but staying positive can make all the difference. Reframe setbacks as temporary obstacles rather than permanent failures. Remind yourself of past successes and the progress you've made. Positive self-talk and affirmations can reinforce your belief in your capabilities and keep you motivated.

I remember another significant setback when a major real estate deal I was working on fell through at the last minute. The deal had been months in the making, and losing it felt like a significant blow. However, instead of giving in to negativity, I reminded myself of the other successful deals I had closed and the positive feedback from satisfied clients. This helped me regain my confidence and continue pursuing new opportunities with renewed determination.

Seeking support from others is also vital in overcoming rejection and setbacks. Surround yourself with a network of supportive friends, family, and mentors who can provide encouragement and perspective. Sharing your experiences and seeking advice can help you see things from a different angle and find new solutions. In my journey, I have been fortunate to have mentors who offered invaluable guidance during tough times. Their support helped me stay focused on my goals and reminded me that setbacks are a natural part of the growth process.

Resilience is built through experience, and each setback is an opportunity to strengthen this essential trait. One way to build resilience is by setting realistic and achievable goals. Break down larger objectives into smaller, manageable tasks, and celebrate each milestone along the way. This approach not only keeps you motivated but also makes setbacks feel less overwhelming. When I set out to establish my own real estate brokerage, I faced numerous challenges. By breaking down the process into smaller steps, such as securing funding, building a client base, and marketing my services, I was able to stay focused and resilient even when faced with setbacks.

Persistence is another key factor in overcoming rejection and setbacks. Success rarely comes overnight, and the path is often fraught with obstacles. Stay committed to your goals, and don't be afraid to try different approaches. If one strategy doesn't work, be willing to adapt and explore new options. When I first started in real estate, I tried various marketing strategies to attract clients. Some failed, but others succeeded. By persisting and continually adapting my approach, I was able to build a successful business over time.

It's also important to take care of your mental and physical well-being during challenging times. Stress and anxiety can take a toll on your health, making it harder to stay motivated and resilient. Practice self-care by engaging in activities that help you relax and recharge, such as exercise, meditation, and spending time with loved ones. Maintaining a healthy lifestyle can improve your ability to cope with stress and bounce back from setbacks.

Lastly, embrace a growth mindset. This concept, popularized by psychologist Carol Dweck, involves viewing challenges and failures as opportunities for growth rather than threats to your self-worth. A growth mindset fosters resilience, curiosity, and a willingness to learn. It encourages you to see setbacks as stepping stones to success rather than insurmountable barriers. Throughout my career, adopting a growth mindset has helped me remain open to new ideas, learn from my experiences, and continuously improve.

Dealing with rejection and setbacks is an inevitable part of any journey toward success. By acknowledging your feelings, learning from experiences, maintaining a positive mindset, seeking support, building resilience, staying persistent, taking care of your well-being, and embracing a growth mindset, you can overcome adversity and continue moving forward. These strategies have helped me navigate numerous challenges in my career and can empower you to turn setbacks into opportunities for growth and success. Remember, it's not the setbacks that define you, but how you respond to them.

CHAPTER FIFTEEN

Balancing Personal Life and Career

In the fast-paced world of real estate, where deals are constantly in motion and clients' needs demand immediate attention, finding an equilibrium between one's personal life and career can feel like an impossible feat. Yet, as I've learned through years of trial and error, this balance is not just achievable—it's essential for long-term success and fulfillment.

When I first dove headfirst into the real estate industry, I was consumed by an insatiable hunger for success. Every waking moment was devoted to chasing leads, closing deals, and building my business. I wore my 80-hour workweeks like a badge of honor, convinced that this relentless grind was the only path to achieving my dreams. Little did I know that this single-minded focus would come at a steep cost—not just to my personal relationships and well-being, but ultimately to the very success I was so desperately pursuing.

It wasn't until I found myself on the brink of burnout, my personal life in shambles and my health deteriorating, that I realized something had to change. This wake-up call set me on a journey of discovery, forcing me to reevaluate my priorities and find a way to thrive both personally and professionally. The lessons I learned along the way have not only transformed my own life but have become the cornerstone of how I mentor and guide the agents on my team.

One of the most crucial realizations I had was that true success isn't measured solely by the number of deals closed or the size of my bank account. Real, lasting success encompasses all aspects of life—health, relationships, personal growth, and yes, career achievements. It's about building a life that's not just financially prosperous but rich in experiences, connections, and meaning.

So, how does one go about striking this delicate balance? It starts with a shift in mindset. Instead of viewing your personal life and career as competing forces, begin to see them as complementary elements of a fulfilling life. When you nurture your personal relationships and well-being, you bring more energy, creativity, and resilience to your work. Conversely, when you achieve professional milestones, it can bring a sense of accomplishment and security that enhances your personal life.

One practical strategy I've found immensely helpful is the implementation of clear boundaries. In the early days of my career, I was always 'on,' responding to emails at midnight and taking client calls during family dinners. I thought this level of availability was necessary to succeed, but in reality, it was eroding the quality of both my work and my personal life.

Now, I set defined work hours and stick to them as much as possible. Outside of these hours, I make a conscious effort to be present with my family and friends. This doesn't mean I never take an important call outside of work hours, but it does mean that these instances are the exception rather than the rule. I've found that clients respect these boundaries when they're clearly communicated, and it actually enhances their perception of me as a professional who values work-life balance.

Technology can be both a blessing and a curse when it comes to maintaining these boundaries. While it allows for greater flexibility in where and when we work, it can also create the expectation of constant availability. I've learned to use technology to my advantage by setting up automated responses during off-hours and using scheduling tools to manage my time more effectively. This allows me to stay connected and responsive without being tethered to my devices 24/7.

Another key aspect of maintaining balance is learning to delegate and build a strong support system. As my business grew, I realized that trying to do everything myself was not only unsustainable but also limiting the potential of my team. By entrusting capable team members with important tasks and responsibilities, I not only freed up more of my own time but also empowered my agents to grow and develop their skills.

This principle extends to my personal life as well. I've learned to ask for help when I need it, whether it's from my spouse, family members, or friends. There's no shame in admitting that you can't do it all alone. In fact, allowing others to support you can strengthen your relationships and create a sense of shared purpose.

One of the most transformative practices I've adopted is regular self-reflection and goal-setting. At the end of each week, I take time to review both my professional and personal accomplishments and challenges. This practice helps me stay aligned with my values and ensures that I'm making progress in all areas of my life, not just in my career.

During these reflection sessions, I ask myself questions like: Did I spend quality time with my loved ones this week? Did I take care of my physical and mental health? Am I feeling fulfilled in my work? This honest self-assessment allows me to make adjustments and course corrections before small imbalances become major issues.

It's important to note that achieving perfect balance every

single day is an unrealistic goal. There will be times when work demands more of your attention, and other times when personal matters take priority. The key is to strive for balance over the long term, understanding that it's okay to have periods of fluctuation as long as you're consistently working towards equilibrium.

One strategy that has helped me navigate these fluctuations is the concept of "seasons" in life and career. Just as nature has different seasons, our lives and careers go through various phases. There may be seasons of intense focus on career growth, followed by seasons where personal life takes center stage. Recognizing and embracing these seasons can alleviate the pressure to maintain perfect balance at all times.

For instance, when I was first building my brokerage, there was a period of several months where I had to pour an enormous amount of energy into getting the business off the ground. During this time, I had honest conversations with my family about the temporary nature of this intense work phase and made sure to carve out small but meaningful moments of connection amidst the chaos.

Once the business was more established, I intentionally shifted into a season of prioritizing family time and personal rejuvenation. This ebb and flow between career focus and personal life focus has allowed me to achieve significant professional milestones while still nurturing my most important relationships.

Another crucial aspect of maintaining work-life balance is taking care of your physical and mental health. In the early days of my career, I often sacrificed sleep, exercise, and proper nutrition in the name of 'hustling.' I thought I was being productive, but in reality, I was diminishing my effectiveness and setting myself up for burnout.

Now, I prioritize my health as a non-negotiable part of my routine. Regular exercise, adequate sleep, and a balanced diet are not luxuries—they're essential investments in my overall well-being and professional performance. I've found that when I take care of my body and mind, I'm more focused, creative, and resilient in both my personal and professional life.

Meditation and mindfulness practices have been game-changers for me in managing stress and maintaining perspective. Taking even just 10 minutes a day to quiet my mind and focus on the present moment has dramatically improved my ability to handle the pressures of a demanding career while staying connected to what truly matters in life.

It's also important to cultivate interests and passions outside of work. While real estate is a huge part of my life, it's not the entirety of who I am. I make a point of pursuing hobbies and activities that have nothing to do with my career. Whether it's reading a novel, playing a sport, or learning a new skill, these pursuits provide a much-needed mental break from work and help me maintain a sense of identity beyond my professional achievements.

One of the most challenging aspects of balancing personal life and career is learning to say "no." In an industry built on relationships and networking, it can feel counterintuitive to turn down opportunities or invitations. However, I've learned that saying no to things that don't align with my priorities is actually saying yes to what matters most.

This doesn't mean becoming a recluse or turning down every social invitation. It's about being selective and intentional with your time and energy. I've developed a simple litmus test for deciding whether to take on new commitments: Will this opportunity bring me closer to my goals (both personal and professional) or pull me further away from them? This clarity has been invaluable in maintaining balance and staying true to my values.

Of course, the journey to achieving work-life balance is not without its challenges and setbacks. There have been times when I've fallen back into old patterns of overworking or neglecting important personal relationships. The key is to approach these moments not with self-judgment, but with curiosity and a commitment to learning and growth.

One particularly difficult period in my life taught me the importance of this balance in a profound way. A few years into building my brokerage, I received news that my father had been diagnosed with a serious illness. At the time, I was in the midst of a major expansion of the business and felt torn between my professional obligations and my desire to be there for my family.

This personal challenge forced me to confront my priorities head-on. I had to make the difficult decision to step back from some of my work responsibilities to spend more time with my father during his treatment. It was a stark reminder that no amount of professional success could replace the precious moments with loved ones.

Navigating this period required open communication with my team and clients. I was surprised by the outpouring of support and understanding I received. Many of my colleagues stepped up to help cover my responsibilities, and clients were incredibly patient and accommodating. This experience reinforced the importance of building strong relationships both in and out of work—when life throws you a curveball, these connections become an invaluable support system.

During this time, I also learned the power of vulnerability in leadership. By being open about my personal struggles with my team, I created a culture where others felt comfortable discussing their own work-life balance challenges. This openness has led to a more supportive and understanding work environment, where we all strive to help each other achieve balance.

The experience with my father's illness also prompted me to implement more flexible work arrangements for my team. I realized that everyone has personal challenges and responsibilities outside of work, and providing flexibility can lead to happier, more loyal, and ultimately more productive employees. This shift not only improved the work-life balance for my team but also gave us a competitive edge in attracting and retaining top talent.

Another personal challenge that significantly influenced my professional decisions came when my spouse was offered a job opportunity in another state. This situation forced us to have serious conversations about our priorities as a family and the future direction of my career.

After much soul-searching, we decided to take the leap and relocate. This meant I had to restructure my business, shifting to a more remote leadership model and trusting my team to handle more day-to-day operations. While this transition was daunting, it ultimately led to tremendous growth—both personally and professionally.

The move pushed me out of my comfort zone and forced me to innovate in how I ran my business. I invested in better technology for remote collaboration, developed new systems for managing a distributed team, and found creative ways to maintain strong client relationships from afar. These changes not only allowed me to support my spouse's career but also opened up new opportunities for expanding my business beyond geographical boundaries.

This experience taught me the importance of being adaptable and open to change. Sometimes, what seems like a challenge to our career can actually be a catalyst for growth and innovation. By prioritizing my personal life and being willing to adapt my professional approach, I was able to achieve a new level of success that I hadn't previously imagined.

One of the most valuable lessons I've learned about balancing personal life and career is the importance of being present in the moment. In our hyper-connected world, it's easy to be physically present but mentally elsewhere—checking emails during family dinner or thinking about work problems while on vacation.

I've made a conscious effort to practice mindfulness and truly engage in whatever I'm doing, whether it's a business meeting or playing with my children. This not only improves the quality of my interactions but also reduces stress and increases overall life satisfaction. When I'm fully present at work, I'm more productive and creative. When I'm fully present with my family and friends, I'm building stronger, more meaningful relationships.

Another crucial aspect of maintaining balance is regular communication with your loved ones about your career goals and challenges. I make it a point to have regular "check-ins" with my spouse and children, discussing not just logistics but also our feelings, aspirations, and concerns. These conversations help ensure that we're all on the same page and that my career decisions are aligned with our family's overall goals and values.

It's also important to involve your family in your success. I make sure to celebrate professional milestones with my loved ones, helping them feel connected to my work life. Whether it's a small celebration dinner for closing a big deal or bringing my kids to the office occasionally, these moments help bridge the gap between my work and personal life.

One strategy that has been particularly effective in maintaining work-life balance is the concept of "non-negotiables." These are the activities or commitments that I refuse to compromise on, no matter how busy work gets. For me, this includes weekly date nights with my spouse, attending my children's important events, and my daily exercise routine. By treating these as sacrosanct, I ensure that my personal life doesn't get swallowed up by work demands.

It's also crucial to remember that work-life balance looks different for everyone. What works for me might not work for you, and that's okay. The key is to find a rhythm that aligns with your personal values, goals, and life circumstances. This might involve some trial and error, but the effort is well worth it.

As leaders in the real estate industry, we have a responsibility not just to achieve balance in our own lives, but to foster an environment that supports work-life balance for our teams. This means leading by example, respecting boundaries, and creating policies that promote a healthy integration of work and personal life.

In my brokerage, we've implemented initiatives like flexible working hours, mental health days, and team-building activities that include families. We also regularly discuss the importance of balance in our team meetings, sharing strategies and supporting each other in our efforts to lead well-rounded lives.

One of the most rewarding aspects of prioritizing work-life balance has been seeing the positive impact it has on my team's performance and satisfaction. When people feel supported in managing their personal lives, they bring more energy, creativity, and commitment to their work. This has translated into better client service, increased productivity, and a more positive work environment overall.

It's important to note that achieving work-life balance is not a one-time accomplishment, but an ongoing process. As our lives and careers evolve, so too must our strategies for maintaining balance. What worked at one stage of your career might not be effective at another. The key is to remain flexible, self-aware, and committed to making adjustments as needed.

As I reflect on my journey in balancing my personal life and career, I'm filled with gratitude for the lessons learned—often the hard way—and the growth that has come from facing these challenges head-on. I'm also inspired by the possibilities that lie ahead, not just for myself but for all of us in the real estate industry.

We have the power to redefine what success looks like, to create careers that enhance rather than detract from our personal lives. It's not always easy, and there will undoubtedly be bumps along the way. But the reward—a life rich in both professional achievement and personal fulfillment—is well worth the effort.

So, I challenge you to take a step back and evaluate your own work-life balance. Are you living in alignment with your values?

Are you making time for the people and activities that truly matter to you? If not, what small step can you take today to move in that direction?

Remember, every great journey begins with a single step. Whether it's setting a new boundary, having an honest conversation with your loved ones, or simply taking a moment to appreciate the present, you have the power to create positive change in your life.

As we navigate the exciting and often unpredictable world of real estate, let's commit to supporting each other in this quest for balance. Let's create a culture where success is measured not just by our professional accomplishments, but by the richness and fulfillment of our lives as a whole.

In doing so, we not only improve our own lives but set an example for future generations of real estate professionals. We show that it's possible to build thriving careers without sacrificing our personal well-being and relationships. And in the end, isn't that the truest measure of success?

So here's to finding that sweet spot where our personal and professional lives not only coexist but enhance each other. Here's to building careers that energize rather than deplete us, and to creating lives filled with purpose, joy, and meaningful connections. The journey may not always be easy, but I can assure you, it's one of the most rewarding adventures you'll ever embark upon.

As we close this chapter, I encourage you to take a moment to envision the balanced life you want to create. What does it look like? How does it feel? Hold onto that vision, let it guide your decisions, and take consistent action towards making it a reality. Remember, you have the power to shape your life and career in a way that brings you true fulfillment. The path to balance starts with a single step—why not take it today?

CHAPTER SIXTEEN

From Dreams to Reality: Action Steps

As we reach the final chapter of this journey, it's time to transform the insights and strategies we've explored into concrete action. The path from where you are now to where you dream of being may seem daunting, but remember - every great achievement begins with a single step.

Your real estate empire won't be built overnight, but it will be built day by day, decision by decision, action by action. This chapter is your roadmap, your call to arms, your catalyst for change. It's time to stop dreaming and start doing.

First and foremost, you need to get crystal clear on your vision. Close your eyes for a moment and really see it - the life you want to create, the impact you want to have, the legacy you want to leave. What does success look like to you? Is it a certain income level? A number of properties in your portfolio? The freedom to travel the world? The ability to give back to your community?

Don't limit yourself here. Dream big. As the saying goes, *"Shoot for the moon. Even if you miss, you'll land among the stars."* Your vision should excite you, maybe even scare you a little. It should pull you forward and give you a reason to push through the inevitable challenges and setbacks.

Once you have that vision, write it down. Make it tangible. Put it somewhere you'll see it every day. This isn't just a feel-good exercise - studies have shown that people who write down their goals are significantly more likely to achieve them. Your written vision becomes your North Star, guiding your decisions and keeping you on track when the going gets tough.

Now that you know where you're going, it's time to plot your course. Break down your big vision into smaller, manageable goals. If your ultimate aim is to own 100 rental properties, what's your goal for this year? For this quarter? For this month?

Remember, these goals should be SMART: Specific, Measurable, Achievable, Relevant, and Time-bound. Instead of *"I want to grow my business,"* try *"I will close 10 residential property deals in the next 6 months."* This gives you a clear target to aim for and a way to measure your progress.

With your goals set, it's time to create your action plan. This is where the rubber meets the road. What specific steps do you need to take to achieve your goals? If your goal is to close 10 deals in 6 months, your action plan might include steps like:

1. Reach out to 20 potential leads per day

2. Attend 3 networking events per month

3. Improve your sales pitch and practice it daily

4. Invest in targeted online advertising

5. Hire a virtual assistant to handle administrative tasks

Be as detailed as possible in your action plan. The more specific you are, the easier it will be to follow through. And don't forget to assign deadlines to each action step. Without deadlines, it's too easy to procrastinate and let opportunities slip by.

Now comes the most crucial part - taking action. All the planning in the world won't get you anywhere if you don't act on it. Start with small, manageable steps. If the idea of calling 20 leads a day feels overwhelming, start with 5. Then 10. Then 15. Build momentum gradually.

Remember, imperfect action is better than perfect inaction. You don't need to have everything figured out before you start. You'll learn and improve as you go. The most successful real estate investors aren't necessarily the ones who know the most - they're the ones who do the most.

As you start taking action, you'll inevitably face obstacles and setbacks. This is where your mindset becomes crucial. Cultivate a growth mindset - view challenges as opportunities to learn and grow, not as failures. When you hit a roadblock, ask yourself, *"What can I learn from this? How can I use this to become better?"*

Resilience is key in this business. There will be deals that fall through, clients who back out, and market fluctuations that catch you off guard. The ability to bounce back from these setbacks will determine your long-term success. Remember, every "no" brings you one step closer to a 'yes.' Every mistake teaches you a valuable lesson that will serve you in the future.

One powerful way to build resilience is to surround yourself with the right people. Jim Rohn famously said, *"You are the average of the five people you spend the most time with."* Look at your circle - are they lifting you up or holding you back? Seek out mentors who have achieved what you want to achieve. Join mastermind groups of like-minded, ambitious individuals. Their energy and success will inspire and motivate you.

At the same time, be wary of negative influences. There will always be naysayers and doubters. Some may be well-meaning friends or family who are concerned about the risks you're taking. Others may be motivated by their own fears or insecurities. Either way, don't let their doubts become your doubts. Believe in yourself and your vision, even when others don't.

As you progress on your journey, it's crucial to track your progress and celebrate your wins, no matter how small. Did you make those 20 calls today? Celebrate it. Did you close your first deal? Celebrate it big time! Too often, we focus on how far we still have to go and forget to acknowledge how far we've come. Recognizing your progress boosts your motivation and reinforces the behaviors that lead to success.

At the same time, be honest with yourself about areas where you're falling short. If you're not hitting your goals, don't make excuses - make changes. Analyze what's not working and adjust your approach. Maybe you need to refine your sales technique. Maybe you need to explore different lead-generation strategies. Maybe you need to delegate more tasks to free up your time for high-value activities.

Continuous learning and improvement should be a cornerstone of your action plan. The real estate market is always evolving, and so should you. Stay updated on market trends, new technologies, and best practices in the industry. Attend seminars, read books, and listen to podcasts. Invest in your own education - it's one of the best investments you can make.

As you start to see success, it's important to maintain balance in your life. Yes, building a real estate empire requires hard work and dedication. But it shouldn't come at the cost of your health, your relationships, or your happiness. Make time for self-care, for your loved ones, for the things that bring you joy outside of work. Success is the sweetest when you have people to share it with.

Remember also to give back as you grow. Not only is it the right thing to do, but it also brings its own rewards. Mentoring new investors, contributing to your community, and supporting causes you believe in - these activities bring a sense of fulfillment that no amount of money can match. Plus, they help you build a positive reputation in the industry, which can lead to more opportunities down the line.

As you implement your action plan, stay flexible. The path to success is rarely a straight line. Be prepared to pivot when necessary. Maybe a strategy that worked well in one market doesn't translate to another. Maybe new regulations change the playing field. Maybe you discover a niche that you're particularly passionate about. Don't be so rigid in your plan that you miss out on unexpected opportunities.

One powerful tool in your action arsenal is the power of habits. Our lives are essentially the sum of our habits. Want to be a successful real estate investor? Develop the habits of successful real estate investors. This might mean waking up early to review market trends, blocking out time each day for lead generation, or setting aside Sunday evenings to plan your week ahead.

Remember, habits take time to form. Be patient with yourself. It typically takes about 66 days for a new behavior to become automatic. Stick with it, even when it's difficult. The compounding effect of good habits over time is truly remarkable.

Another crucial action step is to leverage technology to your advantage. In today's digital age, there are countless tools and platforms that can streamline your operations, improve your marketing, and help you make data-driven decisions. From customer relationship management (CRM) systems to social media marketing tools to property management software, technology can be a game-changer in scaling your business.

However, don't fall into the trap of thinking that technology can replace human connection. Real estate is still very much a people business. Use technology to enhance your relationships, not replace them. A personalized email or a phone call can often be more effective than a mass-marketed message.

As you take action and start seeing results, it's important to regularly reassess and adjust your goals. What seemed ambitious a year ago might now be too easy. Or you might realize that your priorities have shifted. That's okay. Your goals should evolve as you do. The important thing is to always have something you're striving for, something that pushes you to grow and improve.

One often overlooked aspect of taking action is the importance of self-belief. You need to truly believe that you are capable of achieving your goals. If there's a little voice in your head saying *"You can't do this,"* it's time to change that narrative. Affirmations, visualization exercises, and reflecting on past successes can all help boost your self-belief.

Remember, belief isn't about ignoring reality or pretending that challenges don't exist. It's about having confidence in your ability to overcome those challenges. It's about knowing that even if you fail, you have the resilience to get back up and try again.

As you implement your action plan, pay attention to your energy levels. Taking massive action requires significant energy, both mental and physical. Make sure you're fueling yourself properly - eat well, exercise regularly, and get enough sleep. Your body is the vehicle that will carry you to success; treat it with care.

It's also crucial to manage your mental energy. Learn to say no to activities and commitments that don't align with your goals. Protect your time fiercely. Every minute you spend on low-value activities is a minute you're not spending on actions that move you closer to your vision.

One powerful action step is to create systems and processes in your business. This might not seem as exciting as closing deals, but it's crucial for long-term success and scalability. Document your best practices, create checklists for recurring tasks, and establish clear communication protocols. This not only makes your operations more efficient but also makes it easier to delegate tasks as your business grows.

Speaking of delegation, learning to let go and trust others is a crucial step in scaling your business. You can't do everything yourself, and trying to will only lead to burnout. Identify tasks that can be delegated and find reliable people to handle them. This frees you up to focus on high-level strategy and the activities that truly move the needle in your business.

As you take action and start seeing success, be prepared for new challenges. Success often brings increased complexity - more properties to manage, more employees to lead, and more stakeholders to satisfy. Stay humble and be willing to admit when you need help. Seeking advice from those who have navigated similar challenges can save you a lot of time and headaches.

Remember also to stay ethical in all your dealings. In the pursuit of success, it can be tempting to cut corners or bend the rules. Resist this temptation. Your reputation is your most valuable asset in this business. Once lost, it's incredibly difficult to regain. Always operate with integrity, even when it might cost you in the short term.

As you implement your action plan, don't forget to enjoy the journey. Yes, reaching your goals is important, but don't be so focused on the destination that you miss the beauty of the path. Celebrate the small victories, learn from the setbacks, and appreciate the relationships you build along the way. Success is as much about who you become as it is about what you achieve.

In conclusion, the journey from dreams to reality is paved with consistent, purposeful action. It's about setting a clear vision, breaking it down into manageable goals, creating a detailed action plan, and then executing that plan day in and day out. It's about developing the right mindset, building resilience, continually learning, and improving. It's about leveraging technology while maintaining human connections. It's about believing in yourself, managing your energy, creating systems, delegating effectively, and always operating with integrity.

Remember, every successful real estate investor started exactly where you are now. They had dreams, doubts, fears, and obstacles. What set them apart was their willingness to take action despite those doubts and fears. They were willing to fail, learn, adjust, and try again.

Now it's your turn. You have the knowledge, you have the strategies, you have the inspiration. All that's left is to take that first step. And then the next. And the next. Keep moving forward, keep taking action, and I promise you, one day you'll look back and be amazed at how far you've come.

Your journey to real estate success or any other career starts now. Take action, make it happen, and turn those dreams into reality. The future you dream of is waiting for you to create it.

So what are you waiting for? Get out there and make it happen!